INDECENT PHOTOGRAPHER

INDECENT PHOTOGRAPHER

By: Frank Pōmaika'i Munden

Copyright @ Frank Munden 2021
United States Copyright Office
Effective Date: November 8, 2021.
Munden Productions and Publications, LLC.
Honolulu, Hawai'i. First Edition.

Please check out, "Tamehameha Uncensored, Detailed Histories of Hawai'i's First King", by Frank Pōmaika'i Munden. Illustrated by Andy Lee. Edited by Faith Munden. This book covers the history of Tamehameha, from his many birth stories to his death. It also speaks about the fact that Kamehameha is not the name of the King of Hawai'i, but it's really Tamehameha. Munden provides evidence to prove this, including evidence that shows that the Hawaiian language spoken today was altered in the 1820's.

In addition, this book teaches many facts and figures about the ancient Hawaiian people, including multiple wars, such as the Battle of the Bitter Rain, Battle of the Red Mounted Guns and the Battle of the Nu'uanu Pali.

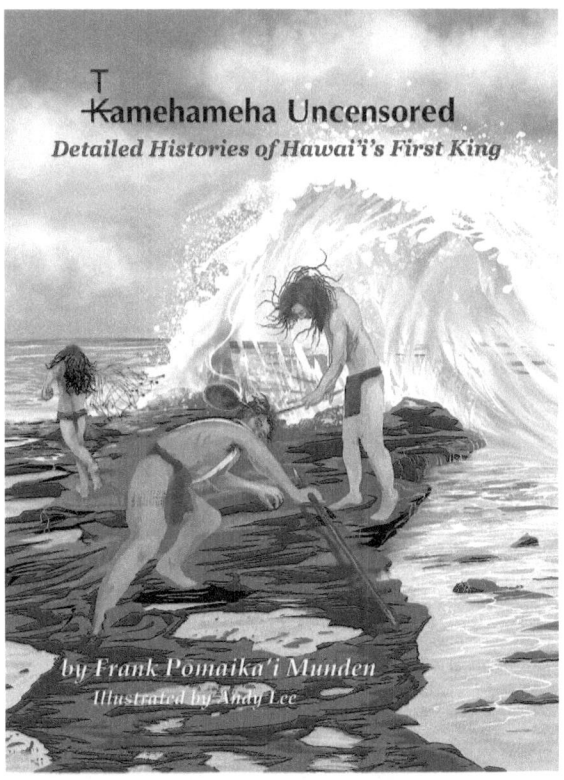

Print book and Kindle E-book available at Amazon.com

Frank Pōmaika'i Munden wrote a second book with his brother Frazier Munden. The book is called, "Love is Deeper Than Skin." It's about a woman who has a burn scar on her face and has to deal with people staring at her. This book can be found on Amazon.com in E-book and Print Form. This book was Illustrated by Andy Lee and features the editing team of Robert Means, Angel (Garcia) Wyatt, James Giroux and Richard Concepcion.

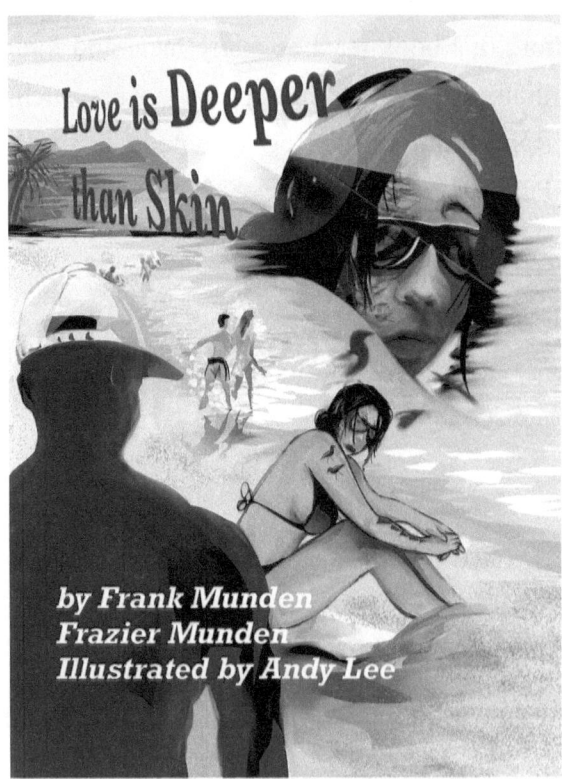

Print book and Kindle E-book can be found on Amazon.com

Frank Pōmaika'i Munden's third book, "The Central American Drug Ship", can also be found on Amazon.com in E-book and Print Form. It's about a man, named Reggae, who spend time in the US Navy and now deals with PTSD and other serious issues from an incident that happened in Sept 1990 off Central American Waters. It also talks about Reggae's time in the Navy, including racism and adventures that came from his enlistment. It was illustrated by Andy Lee and features the editing team of Pam Calilao, Richard Concepcion, James Giroux, Aladdin El-Kadi and Angel (Garcia) Wyatt.

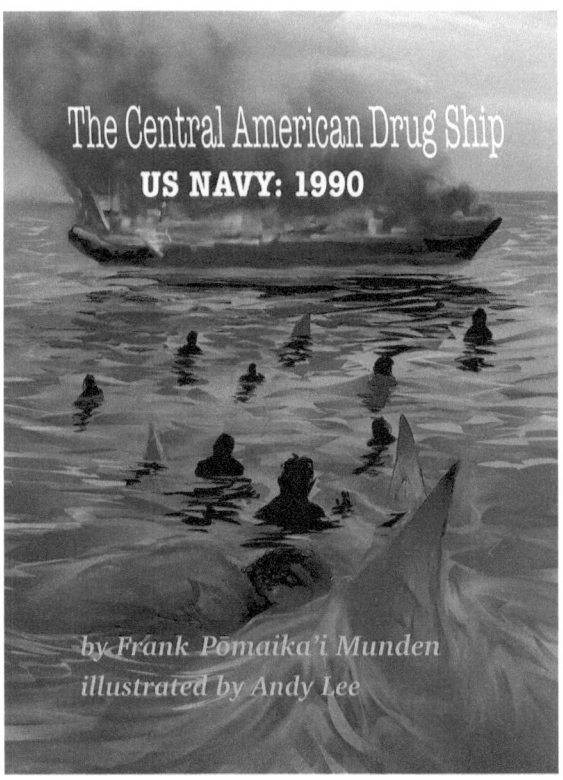

Print book and Kindle E-book can be found on Amazon.com

Dedicated to my parents Frank Munden Sr. (RIP),
Faith Munden (RIP). Brothers: Forest Munden;
Frazier Munden. Jenell "Ke'alohi" Sato and
God daughter: Taylor Meleanaka'aiakamanu King.

Table of Context

Chapter 1: Jessica's Photo Shoot .... 1.
Chapter 2: Photo Options .... 9.
Chapter 3: Gina's Upbringing .... 15.
Chapter 4: Gina's Photo Shoot .... 19.
Chapter 5: Confrontation on the Beach .... 27.
Chapter 6: The Deception. .... 35.
Chapter 7: More Photo Sharing .... 45.
Chapter 8: Photos around the World .... 49.
Chapter 9: The Detective, Lawyer and Real Photographer .... 57.
Chapter 10: Epilogue .... 69.
Author's Bibliography: Frank Munden .... 75.
Illustrator's Bibliography: Andy Lee .... 77.
Editor's Bibliography: Pam Calilao. .... 79.
Editor's Bibliography: James Giroux. .... 81.
Editor's Bibliography: Bo Daniel Mandoe .... 83.
Editor's Bibliography: Angel (Garcia) Wyatt .... 85.
Author's Last Words .... 87.
Special Thanks .... 89.

Warning: For mature readers only. Story contains descriptions of nudity in photography and strong language. It's not intended for underage or immature readers. It's based off a blending of true stories. Names, identities and ethnicities in this story have been changed and altered for privacy. Any names, descriptions or looks featured in this story are fictional and not based off of any living person.

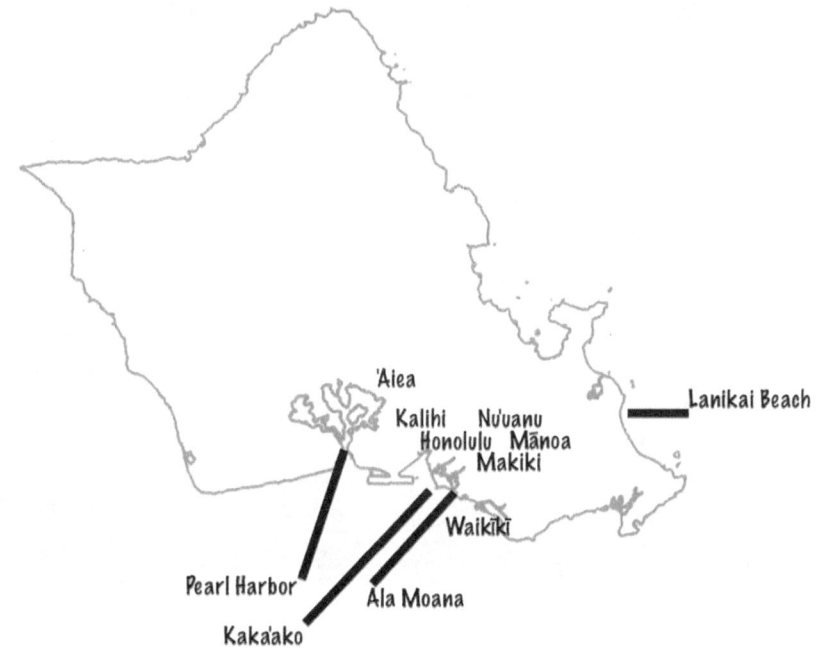

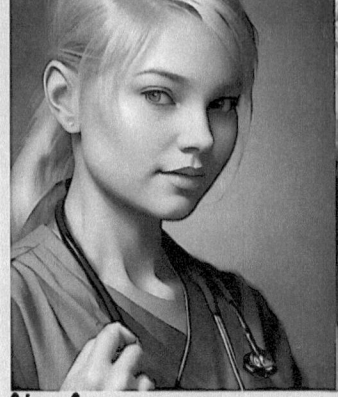
Gina Grey

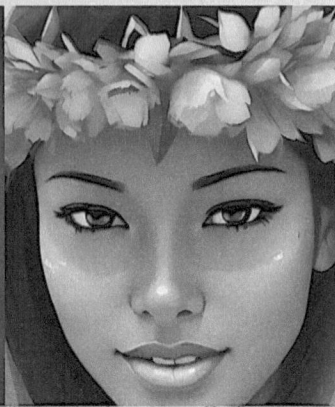
Jessica Cromwell-Tanner

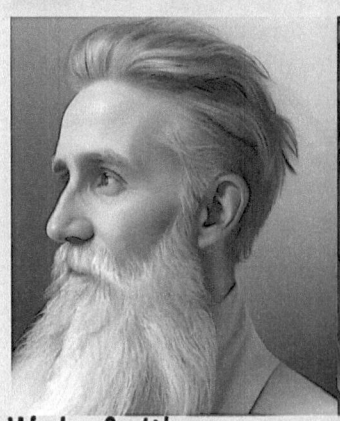
Wesley Smith

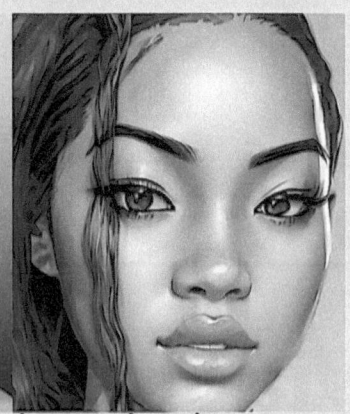
Amanda Crenshaw

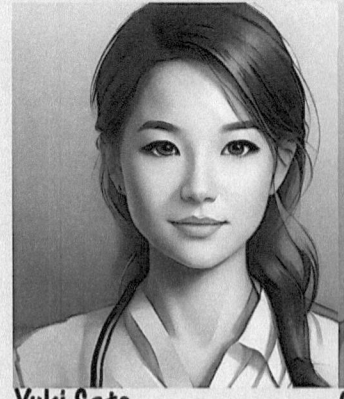
Yuki Sato

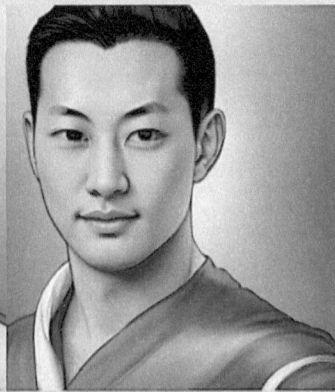
Clarence Sato

Jessica's Photo Shoot

In military housing, only a few minutes from Joint Base Pearl Harbor-Hickam, Hawai'i, 25 year-old Jessica Hōkūlani Cromwell-Tanner is rearranging some photos on her laptop. She received these photos last night from a photographer she recently met online. Five days ago, Jessica participated in a photo shoot, at her home, with a photographer that was offering discounted photography services. For several months, Jessica wanted to do a photo shoot, but never found the time to do it because of her busy schedule as a registered nurse.

Jessica particularly wanted to do this photo shoot to surprise her 27 year-old husband, Petty Officer 2nd. Class Franklin Tanner. Tanner is serving on the USS Chung-Hoon (DDG-93) as a Machinist Mate. Jessica hasn't seen her husband for almost three months now. She really misses him. (The Chung-Hoon is a Destroyer stationed out of Joint Base Pearl Harbor-Hickam, but is currently in Japanese waters.)

Originally, Jessica just wanted to be photographed in several evening gowns and a couple of conservative/non-revealing lingerie. However, in the excitement of her photo shoot session, Jessica uncharacteristically let go of her inhibitions and took several photos way beyond what she originally planned on taking.

Jessica was born in a Naval hospital in San Diego. She's used to being around Navy life, since her father, John Kānekoa Cromwell, a man with Caucasian and Hawaiian ancestry, served over 30 years in the Navy and retired as a Chief Warrant Officer. Jessica and her Filipina mother, Isabella, were used to moving from duty station to duty station every time Jessica's father reenlisted. Jessica didn't mind the adventure of moving every so many years and loved the fact that she got to live on bases in San Diego, Scotland, Virginia, Japan and then Hawai'i. Jessica even boasts that she got to graduate from a high school, in Hawai'i, with only vowels in its name. (Aiea High School.)

When Jessica announced that she was getting married to Franklin Tanner three years ago, it was no surprise to anyone that she would marry military. It made her mother and father very proud. (Franklin Tanner is primarily African-American, but has a fractional amount of Caucasian and Cherokee.)

Since Jessica is part-Hawaiian and could prove it on birth certificates going back generations, she got grants and scholarships that fully covered her way through nursing school at the University of Hawai'i at Mānoa. Shortly after nursing school and passing a test, she obtained her current job on a cardiac floor. She likes her job at the hospital, but loves her co-workers even more, including a fellow night shift nurse and best friend, Gina Grey. (Gina and Jessica were nursing classmates at the University of Hawai'i.) At this moment, Jessica is awaiting Gina's arrival to view her photos and to get advice on them.

Jessica hears her cell-phone chime, indicating she just got a text. She looks down and reads a text from Gina saying that she just parked on street and is almost at her door. With a big smile, Jessica goes to the door and opens it up after Gina playfully knocks.

After a friendship hug, Gina comes in and takes off her shoes. This is a Hawai'i custom, since most Hawai'i residents know it's considered rude and unsanitary to wear your footwear into a house and track outside germs, dirt, animal feces or other entities into someone's home. Gina sits down on a sofa and is offered a choice of water, apple juice or iced tea. Gina chooses the iced tea.

After Jessica gives her 27 year-old blond hair, hazel-eyed friend a tall glass of iced tea, Gina asks Jessica how her day off is going.

Jessica says, "It's nice to have a day off after three 12 hour night shifts in a row."

"I know," replies Gina. "It's like the schedulers don't know what it's like to work night shift."

Jessica says, "I doubt if they do. Night shift is no joke. There's a reason why they call the night shift the graveyard shift. It's scientifically proven to take years off your life if you stay on it too long."

"You're absolutely right," says Gina.

Jessica sighs, "Well, hopefully this will be my last series of three 12 hour night shifts in a row. I hope we both get approved to shift over to day shift."

Gina looks puzzled, "I guess you didn't read your email last week. Seo-Yeon approved both of us for day shift. We will no longer be vampires. We will be starting day shift next schedule."

Jessica jumps up in the air and screams.

"I'm so happy! My prayers have been answered! Seo-Yeon's the best manager ever. Soon I'll be able to get some real sleep."

"I know," Gina says with a big smile. "If I wasn't approved, I was going to have my doctor write a note saying how night shift was negatively affecting my health and that I need to shift to daytime hours of employment. If I gave that letter to human resources and the union, the hospital would have no choice but to move me to day or evening shifts and off of night shift."

Jessica says, "I didn't know you could do that."

"If you have a doctor's note, with the right wording, you can with our company. Amanda Crenshaw recently got off night shift that way. Well she deserved it after five years of straight night shift work," says Gina.

"I know Yuki Sato gets Sunday off since she had a doctor's note saying she needs that day off for religious purposes," says Jessica.

"I'm the one who encouraged Yuki to get that doctor's note. I know how much God and her faith mean to her," says Gina.

"Well I guess that's why you're a union steward," says Jessica. "And you do a great job at it."

"Thanks," says Gina. "Sometimes I want to quit being a union steward though, especially around contract negotiations. It's hard going up against actual lawyers like Yuki's uncle."

"Well I hope you don't quit. The nurses need people like you watching out for our rights," says Jessica.

"Mahalo," (Thank you), says Gina.

After a few more minutes of small talk about work, Jessica starts showing Gina some of her digital pictures from her photo shoot. Gina is highly impressed by them.

Gina says, "I love these, they're so professionally done."

Jessica smiles, then replies, "Mahalo. You're the first person and the only person, besides my husband, that I'm planning on showing them to. I'm going to email some of them to him later tonight."

"He's going to love them. By the way, when is he coming back to Hawai'i?"

"He's not sure yet, but his ship just left Japan and is heading to Guam. He said once he knows when he's coming back to Hawai'i, he will let me know."

"Cool," says Gina.

Gina and Jessica continue to look at the photos. Gina comments that she likes the evening gowns that Jessica selected, but continues to comment how much she loves the shots taken by the photographer. She also comments how beautiful Jessica looks in the photos. After looking over all the evening gown photos and then a few tame lingerie photos, Gina inquires about the digital photos Jessica is hesitant about showing her husband.

"So where are the photos you are not sure about showing Franklin?"

Jessica's smile turns into hesitancy. Inside, Jessica is starting to feel regret in mentioning to Gina about the photos, she's debating to show her husband, because of the nature of the photos.

Jessica says, "Since you're my best friend in all the world, I got to be honest with you. In a few of these photos, you can see my chest and butt. I didn't take any pornographic style photos, but they are still nudes. Can you handle seeing these type of photos and not thinking of me in a different light?"

Gina asks, "As long as they are not straight out pornography, I won't have a problem."

Jessica answers, "Well, most of the photos I am going to show you are implied nudes, however, I do have a few artistic nudes and about a dozen photos where I am taking a shower and you can see my nude body from the back and side through the glass shower door. In a few of the photos, you can see my chest."

"Okay," says Gina nonchalantly.

Jessica continues, "I guess I got caught up in the moment when I posed for these photos and took Wesley's coaching. He was 100% respectful of my boundaries and told me, "I will only take pictures up to your comfort level. If you feel uncomfortable in any way, please tell me. I will not shoot anything you don't want me to shoot. And he kept to that promise."

"That's good of him to keep his promise," says Gina. "It was," replies Jessica.

Jessica pauses for a second, then continues, "So we started off in evening gowns, then to tame lingerie. After that, I asked him if I could put on a couple of borderline tame lingerie and he said it was up to me. After taking these photos, I decided to break out some lingerie that was a little more revealing in nature. Wesley kept on complimenting how good I looked and that made me feel like I was a super model. Again, I guess I just got caught up in the moment. Without asking, I changed into my sexiest lingerie and didn't even care that the chest area of my lingerie was see through."

Gina says, "Okay."

Jessica continues, "Without even thinking about it, I started just changing from outfit to outfit right in front of him. When I realized we went over an hour, I told him I have to stop because I only have enough money for one hour of his time. He nonchalantly told me not to worry about the time and he will only charge me for an hour no matter how long we took, since he was retiring anyway. The whole photo shoot took almost three hours, but it only felt like maybe 90 minutes."

"That's nice of him to only charge you for an hour," says Gina.

"It was," replies Jessica.

"How much did he charge you?"

Jessica replies, "$150 dollars."

"Sounds extremely cheap for the quality I saw so far," says Gina.

"Throughout the photo shoot, I didn't feel threatened by him in any way. Wesley made me feel very safe and comfortable. I mean, he's around 70 years old and looks like a skinny Santa Claus."

"With the Santa beard too?"

Jessica laughs, "Yes, Santa beard and snow white hair... I started taking implied nude photos with a white sheet draped on me to cover up my naked body. After multiple implied nude photos throughout the apartment, I started taking completely nude artistic style photos. I asked him not to photograph my private area in any of the photos and Wesley honored that. I could tell he went out of his way to avoid taking those type of photos."

"Nice," says Gina.

"After several artistic nudes, we ended the photo shoot with me being in the shower. Wesley suggested it and I trusted him. Throughout the photo shoot, he really made me feel special and valued my input."

"That's great," says Gina.

"After Wesley left, I felt really good about the photo shoot. However that night, I started feeling guilty, like I did something wrong. I should of kept to the plan and just did a shoot with the gowns and tame lingerie. I'm worried what my husband will say if I show him all the photos. Knowing him, I think he would have been okay if the photographer was a woman, but doing nude photography with a man will more than likely upset him. That's why I am debating what photos to show him and which ones I should keep to myself. Or maybe I might just show him and say a female photographer took them. I don't know. What would you do if you were me?"

Gina drops her eyes to the ground, then shakes her head. She says, "This is not an easy decision. Look, if you trust me, let me see the photos and I'll let you know what I think. You don't have to show me all the photos. Just show me what you are comfortable with. Then I can give you my honest opinion."

Jessica pauses for a moment.

Gina says, "I promise I will not tell anyone about these photos or that they even exist."

Jessica says, "I know you wouldn't say anything. It's just that I have a couple of body flaws I'm ashamed of."

Gina laughs a little, then says, "We see naked people every day at work, so don't worry. By now, I've seen thousands of naked people in my life. You have too. Plus, we all have body flaws, I know I do."

"You are right. Everyone has body flaws," says Jessica.

Photo Options

CHAPTER 2

Jessica stirs up the courage and shows Gina two dozen implied nude photos of herself. Gina comments that they are very beautiful. Jessica, feeling less ashamed, shows her the rest of the photos, including the artistic nudes and shower photos. Gina doesn't even flinch when seeing them.

Gina says, "These photos are excellent. They are very tastefully done. This photographer is very talented. I love every picture he has taken of you. And I don't see any body flaws you claim you have."

"Thank you, but what should I do concerning my husband and these photos?"

Gina pauses, then says, "I have no idea what you should do. Knowing your husband, I'm pretty sure he will be upset that you took nude photos with a male photographer, instead of a female."

Jessica sighs, "I'm pretty sure too. At first, I was looking for a female photographer, but when I saw that Wesley was offering a discount on the internet last week, I chose the cheap route verses my gut feeling. Plus, I didn't preplan that I would take nude photos or be naked in front of a photographer. It just happened because Wesley wasn't a threat and he's so friendly."

"I get it," says Gina. "I've taken nude photos before in my life, so I know how it is to get caught up in the moment. It's not uncommon to get carried away in a photo shoot. The last time I took nude photos was with my now ex-husband a couple of years ago. Before I divorced him because of his out of control gambling issues, I grabbed the digital camera, memory cards and flash drives with my nude photos and kept it for myself. I didn't want him to take it and end up on those, 'ex-wife or girlfriend revenge type of sites.' With the amount of anger he had when we divorced, I wouldn't have been surprised if he would have posted such photos. Now we are cordial to each other for the sake of my son."

Jessica says, "It's nice that you guys are now cordial... For my situation, I really don't want to lie, but if I tell the truth, Franklin's going to be very upset I got naked in front of another man and took these photos. He doesn't understand nudity like we do. As you said earlier, we see naked bodies everyday at work. I guess that's why being naked in front of a photographer wasn't such a big deal to me at the time."

"I understand where you are coming from Jessica. Plus you said Wesley was an older man, so you felt that he was harmless."

"Yes he looks like someone's great grandpa."

Gina and Jessica share a brief laugh.

Gina says, "Although in the future, since you are married, you need to be more mindful of who you get naked in front of, unless it's a medical setting of course. You know what I'm saying?"

"I do."

Jessica and Gina have an awkward pause for a moment before Gina offers up possible solutions.

Gina says, "Why don't we look at your options. The first option, you could just be honest with Franklin and show him all the photos. Second option, you can show him all the tame photos and say a male photographer took them, and delete the rest. A third option, you could show him all the photos and say a female photographer took it."

"Hmm...Okay, so which one should I pick?"

"I'm not sure. If I were married like you are, I wouldn't have selected a male photographer for this type of photography in the first place. I would have selected a female."

Jessica says sarcastically, "Well you're a big help. Maybe I'll just choose option four."

"What's option four?"

Jessica says with a little anger, "Don't show him any of the photos and pretend this photo shoot never happened."

Gina, caught off guard, says, "Look I'm sorry. I didn't mean to sound disrespectful or scold you in any way."

Jessica pauses, then replies, "No, I'm sorry Gina. You are trying to help me and I'm the one being disrespectful. I'm just so stressed about this and don't know what to do."

Gina hugs Jessica tight.

"I get it," says Gina.

Jessica starts to cry.

"Look Jessica, you didn't do anything horrible. You're not a bad person. While you possibly had a lapse in judgement, at least you didn't sleep with him...You didn't sleep with Santa Claus did you?"

"No, not at all," says Jessica with a serious tone.

"Well okay, do some thinking, sleep on it, think about it some more and then make your decision. You have a little time to figure this out because your husband is still somewhere between Japan and Guam."

"Ok, thank you."

Jessica and Gina ease out of the photography conversation and into a conversation about a recent date Gina was on with a physical therapist from another hospital. She met this guy through a mutual female friend. (Prior to their date, Gina's friend told her that this man just moved to Hawai'i from Los Angeles two months ago.)

Gina says, "So as the date went on, I realized he was really self-centered and had a type-A, aggressive personality. He kept on talking about all his accomplishments in life and barely asked anything about myself. The final straw for me was when the food came out. He ordered a rib eye steak medium and the steak came out medium rare. This guy yells at the poor waitress to the point that everyone stopped talking in the restaurant and turned towards us. I was so embarrassed. He rudely tells her to look at the steak and tell him if the steak looked medium. The elderly waitress stops and says she thinks it looks medium, but if he wants, she can take it back and make it right. For some odd reason, the guy gets upset with her comment and calls her stupid."

Jessica says, "That's horrible."

"I know. At that point, I could not keep silent. I grabbed his arm and told him that this isn't the Mainland where being rude and yelling at people is much more acceptable and commonplace. I told him that his behavior is considered very rude here in Hawai'i. I then told him to apologize to the waitress. He reluctantly apologized and had the waitress take back the steak. I told him that the waitress had nothing to do with the way the steak was cooked and he shouldn't have spoken to her that way. For some reason unknown to me, he didn't seem to get it. I tried to explain to him that his food's probably going to get spit on by the cook, rubbed on the counter or something worse. He insisted that people don't do that, but I told him otherwise."

Jessica says, "I can't stand type-A aggressive people like that... What happened next?"

Gina says, "Since I am a notoriously quick eater, I decided to wait for his dish to arrive before I ate my mahi mahi plate. After only five minutes of waiting, the guy started complaining that his food was taking a long time. I looked at my watch, then told him that it's only been five minutes, plus chances are that the cook might of had to fire up a new steak. The guy kept on complaining, so after ten more minutes, I asked the waitress to please bring me a take out container and the check for my food and drink.

"When the waitress arrived with a container and the check, the guy asked me what I was doing. I told him that I couldn't take his complaining and his rude behavior anymore. After I paid my check, with a good tip, I told the guy that I would walk home, since I lived only a few minutes from the restaurant. My date said he could give me a ride, but I declined. I walked home and haven't spoken to him ever since."

"So did you tell your friend what happened?"

"Yes I did. She said that at work, he seemed like a nice person with the patients, but she now can see how he does have a type-A like personality. She apologized for the mistake."

"Oh wow," says Jessica.

After more small talk, Jessica and Gina go out and eat sushi at a local restaurant.

Gina's Upbringing

CHAPTER

27 year-old Gina Kehau Grey was born on the island of Maui and raised in the town of Ha'ikū on a ten acre lot. She grew up in a plantation style three bedroom wooden house that's tucked away between a multitude of various fruit trees, ti leaf plants and a flowing stream that has a private waterfall. Inside the stream are freshwater prawns, crayfish and thousands of guppies. Due to ancient Hawaiian customs, Gina's house has several green ti leaf plants planted on all four corners of her house and the entire property has green and red ti leaf plants planted all over the place to keep evil spirits away.

Gina's parents, Sarah and William, raised Gina and her younger brother Robert off of Sarah's hair styling job in Kahului and William's medical marijuana farm. All William's marijuana is grown in a large grow house that's well-guarded by surveillance systems and four adult pit bulls. William also sells mangos, bananas, avocados, coffee beans, cherry guavas and lychee. He owns a shotgun and pistol to guard his crops, but has never had to use them. He has five employees that are all related to him. They are well-paid for what they do on the farm. People in the neighborhood know what William is growing, but don't mess with his crops because of William's Hawaiian ancestry and what's on Gina's land itself.

According to Gina's DNA tests, Gina is 3/4 European, (English, Irish, Scottish, German, Dutch and French), 1/8 Chinese and 1/8

Hawaiian. Of all her ethnicities, her Hawaiian ancestry is the one she thinks of the most. One of Gina's Hawaiian ancestors was a body guard to the first king of Hawai'i, the great Tamehameha (Kamehameha.) In 1810, when the entire Hawaiian Islands became unified under Tamehameha, Tamehameha gave one of his body guards, named Kaleohano, 110 acres of land in Ha'ikū. Over the next 200 years, 100 of the 110 acres were sold to Westerners for a small fraction of the real value.

Concerning the remaining ten acres, this parcel holds the graves of Kaleohano and many of his descendants. It also has a sacrificial heaiu (temple) on a hill that's mostly intact. An elderly Hawaiian kahuna came out one day and said that according to ancient chants and legends, possibly hundreds or thousands of kauwā or Hawaiian slaves were killed and sacrificed at this site.

Gina and her family caretake the heaiu and the graves out of respect for their ancestors, the poor slaves sacrificed here and the ancient Hawaiian culture. About 2-3 times a year, trusted relatives and friends come to the heiau to help clean up and preserve it. (The heiau, like Gina's family home, has green ti leaf plants surrounding the four corners of it.)

Growing up, Gina learned hula, Hawaiian history and culture and is semi-fluent in the Hawaiian language. (She speaks Hawaiian at about a seventh grade level.) She still keeps learning Hawaiian each and every day, including some Hawaiian from Ni'ihau, which still use the T's in their language. She recently learned the words, "aloha katahiaka" (good morning) and "maita'i" (good/fine) from a Hawaiian woman originally from Ni'ihau, but now lives on Kaua'i. Even though Gina looks practically 100% Caucasian, her heart and mind is 100% Hawaiian when it comes to preserving Hawaiian land and the Hawaiian culture.

Indecent Photographer

Gina grew up with a Caucasian mother that's a practicing nudist. Gina's mother Sarah goes nude almost every chance she can. While Gina's dad is conservative in nature and doesn't practice nudity, he respects and allows his wife to be who she wants to be. Gina and her brother grew up swimming naked in her waterfall and Little Beach, Makena (An unofficial nudist beach on Maui.)

Gina was taught that the naked body is something to be celebrated and not to be ashamed of. However, when Gina started reaching puberty, she stopped going nude at Little Beach because she knew some of her male classmates liked to go to this beach to peek at any nude women they could see. A couple of them saw Gina's mother naked at the beach and teased Gina at school about it. Gina dealt with the teasing and didn't let their attitudes change her view of nudity. She did tell her mother about the teenagers teasing her. Gina's mother compromised to help her daughter out and would only go out to Little Beach during school hours and never during spring or summer break.

Gina currently has a three year old son named Nalu. She had him with her now ex-husband Palani. Her son Nalu is a mixed-race child with 5/8 European-American, 1/8 Hawaiian and a fractional amount of Filipino, Spanish, Chinese and Japanese ancestry. In a court order, Palani and Gina have a 60/40 time share in favor of Gina. When it's Palani's time to watch Nalu, he frequently has his mother, Lokelani, watch him since he works long hours at an auto body shop painting cars. Gina is fine with Lokelani watching Nalu, since Lokelani loves Nalu with all her heart and really pays attention to him.

Gina has 100% physical custody of Nalu, meaning that Gina's apartment is the official place of residence for Nalu. When Gina's at work and it's her turn to watch him, she takes Nalu over to her first cousin Sheryl's house. Sheryl is a professional babysitter and watches up to four children with her mother. Luckily, Sheryl lives only ten minutes drive from Gina's apartment near the University of Hawai'i at Mānoa.

Palani pays a very small amount of child support. 50% of that money goes into a college trust fund Nalu will be able to access once he's 18 and graduated high school. Gina actually contributes a much higher amount in a separate college fund and will let Nalu know the breakdown when he's of age to access the accounts.

Gina calls Jessica the next day to inquire how she's doing. Jessica says that she decided to show only the evening gown photos to her husband and hide the rest deep in her computer. Jessica tells Gina that her husband and herself have a rule that they will respect each other's privacy and not look at each other's cell-phone, computer, lap top or anything in the opposite person's personal filing cabinets. It's a rule that hasn't been broken even once.

Gina respects Jessica's decision, then asks for the number of the photographer. Jessica gives it to her and asks if she's planning on doing similar photos that she took with Wesley. Gina says she's seriously thinking about it and will let her know if she gets ahold of Wesley.

Gina's Photo Shoot

CHAPTER

After getting off the phone with Jessica, Gina goes to her computer, in her two bedroom apartment in Waikīkī and looks up Wesley on the internet. She locates his photography site. It has multiple photos with female models. (Gina quickly notices there are no male models on the page.) She's highly impressed with the quality of the photos and notices two photos of Jessica Cromwell-Tanner in a couple of evening gown dresses. Gina sees a fair amount of pictures of models in regular clothing. She also sees a lot of bikini, implied nudes, tame lingerie shots and a handful of photos with blurs around the models exposed breasts. Gina's impressed and decides to call Wesley's number for a photo shoot appointment.

The next morning, Wesley appears at Gina's door of her apartment. He's wearing a red flowered aloha shirt, blue jeans shorts and slippers (flip-flops.) Jessica's description of him was correct. (He does look like a skinny version of Santa Claus.) Gina meets him at the door in a long casual T-shirt and volleyball shorts.

Wesley says with a big smile, "Hello, I'm Wesley Smith."

"Hi, I'm Gina. Come in."

Wesley takes off his slippers at the door entrance and walks in. He carries a very expensive camera and lens in his camera bag. When he sits down on the couch, he's immediately offered a choice of water, coffee or iced tea. Wesley asks for water.

Gina gives an ice cold glass of water to Wesley.

"Mahalo," says Wesley.

"A'ole pilikea," (you're welcome, aka, no trouble), replies Gina.

Gina leads Wesley into her apartment. Wesley immediately scans the room for shots he can take before sitting down on a couch. Gina sits down next to him. Wesley then asks Gina what kind of shots Gina is looking to take today. Gina tells Wesley that she wants to start with some hula shots outdoors on the ground floor of the building in front of some ti leaf plants. After that, she wants to come back to the apartment and do some implied nude and artistic nude shots similar to what her friend Jessica took. Included in the artistic nude poses are a few yoga poses, since Gina loves yoga. Gina then says she wants to take a few shots in the bathtub with rose petals floating in the water.

Gina asks Wesley if she can show him some photo examples that she wants.

With a warm friendly smile, Wesley says, "Yes let me see your ideas. I welcome it. I will shoot whatever photos you want me to shoot. I'm open to shooting anything."

"Okay good," replies Gina.

Gina shows him examples of some of the shots she wants to take on her cell-phone. Gina took these pictures off the internet. Wesley takes out a note pad and makes very quick stick figure sketches.

"I love them. You seemed to be very prepared. Are you a professional model?"

"I never did modeling formally, but I've been photographed many times in my life. And I've done nude photography a few times before, so nudity doesn't bother me. I'm assuming nudity doesn't bother you?"

Wesley laughs, "We are all born naked, so we shouldn't worry so much about nakedness, except if you look like me."

Gina laughs a little, then says, "Wait right here, I'm going to go get changed."

Wesley says, "Okay hold on, before we begin, I always ask my clients to sign a contract." Wesley takes out a contract from his camera bag. It's 14 pages thick and is in small wording.

Wesley hands it over to Gina for her to sign with a pen.

Displaying a warm smile, Wesley says, "Please sign on page 14."

Gina looks very confused and overwhelmed.

"Um...I have to go get my glasses. The words of this contract are small and very numerous."

"Oh don't worry about what it says. It basically says you give me money, I give you photos."

Gina pauses for a moment, then says, "Okay, I trust you."

Without even glancing through the contract, Gina signs it and hands it to Wesley. Wesley nods in approval. He signs it. Wesley then brings out a second contract, exactly the same as the first and has Gina sign that one. After she signs the copy, he gives her one of the copies and smiles. Gina goes to her room to change.

Once Gina is changed, Gina and Wesley go downstairs to the courtyard to take photos near a plumeria tree and a row of green and red ti leaf plants. Gina is wearing a pink and green lokelani haku lei on her head, a red wrap around kapa cloth around her chest and upper waist area and a green pā'ū skirt. (A pā'ū skirt is a traditional kapa skirt originally worn by Ancient Hawaiians.) Wesley loves the color scheme and the way Gina poses.

"Wow you're a natural at this," says Wesley.

Gina replies, "Mahalo."

After 20 minutes of posing in various hula poses, Wesley and Gina go upstairs to work on the next set of photos. Before Wesley can even say anything about Gina changing out of her hula clothes to work on her implied nude shots, Gina stripped down naked in front of him and goes under a razor thin white sheet on her bed. The sheet is slightly see through. Wesley keeps a professional poker-faced look.

Wesley takes multiple photos of Gina using the sheet. Wesley then asks her to take the sheet off and cover up her breasts and private area. Gina does so without hesitation.

"I feel like you're a professional model. Are you sure you haven't done paid modeling work before?"

"No I've never done paid modeling," replies Gina.

"I see…Well I love photographing people who know what they want and just do it without hesitation. It makes it so much easier for me to shoot."

"And I love your photography style. Where did you learn how to shoot so well?"

"While growing up in Florida, my parents bought me a cheap camera when I was four and told me to 'knock myself out.' I love taking pictures of anything and everything. I even took photos of large gators in canals and other waterways, with my parents at my side of course."

"Gators, that's gutsy of you."

"It's not too bad if you keep your distance and stay at an elevated level from them. I would always zoom in on them from a safe distance. I didn't want to take a chance in being a gator's next meal. And my dad always carried a firearm on him when we went out to photograph gators."

"That's smart."

"I agree. Anyways, as I got a little older, my parents moved my two older sisters and myself to Washington State. They wanted to be near my mother's side of the family. My uncle, who owned a photography studio, asked me to come to the studio and learn from him. I watched him photograph all kinds of people from all walks of life. At age 15, I started photographing some of his clients, mostly portraits or family photos.

"Once I turned 18 and graduated high school, I got drafted to go to Vietnam. Luckily, when I went for my Army physical, the doctor found tiny fractional bone spurs in my right foot I never knew I had. The doctor, one of my father's drinking buddies, asked me if I wanted to go to Vietnam or college? I laughed and said I'd would rather go to college of course.

"A couple of months later, I enrolled in a community college in Northern California and took a few pre-law classes. At the time, I wanted to be a lawyer, but soon realized I could make a lot of money in photography, since I have a natural God given gift and eye for this type of work. I dropped out of college at age 20, moved to Hawai'i with my now deceased wife and started a photography business. Other than an occasional trip here and there, I haven't left Hawai'i ever since."

"Oh wow. Sorry about your wife."

"It's okay. She died of natural causes a few years ago...Lung cancer. I told her to stop smoking cigarettes, but she wouldn't listen... Did you know that at one point in history, cigarette companies promoted smoking as healthy?"

"No I didn't. That's terrible."

"Yeah it is. Look it up sometime on the internet. I'm amazed cigarettes and cigars are still legal. It kills people, plain and simple, just like alcohol and illegal drugs...I'm sorry, where's my head. I don't want to ruin this photo shoot over my philosophies and personal opinions."

"It's okay," says Gina. "I'm a nurse, so I get it. I see the negative effects of drugs, cigarettes and alcohol all the time on the cardiac floor."

"Mahalo for your understanding Gina."

"No problem."

Wesley sighs, tears up a little, then says, "Over the last 50 years I've been here, I learned so much about photography and human behavior. I found that it's a blessing from God if you can make money on a job that you absolutely love doing. That is this job. I love taking photos and ironically, you are the last person I am going to photograph before hanging up my lens professionally. I'm going back to Washington State to enjoy my retirement soon. I have a rich brother up there that has three houses on nine acres. He's letting me live in one of the houses that has a flowing stream and all I have to do is pay the utilities and yearly property tax for the house and I'm good to go."

"Lucky man. On my parent's property in Ha'ikū, Maui, there is a flowing stream and a waterfall. I was so blessed to have that growing up. My mom used to take photos of my dad, younger brother and me at the waterfall all the time. She still does when I go over there 3-4 times a year. When I go there, I usually take my son Nalu. He loves the water a lot."

"How old is your son?"

"He's three years old."

"Nice," says Wesley. "I have two sons in their 40's and five grandchildren."

"Cool."

Wesley takes several more implied nude photos of Gina throughout her home. He then works with Gina in taking some artistic nude photos by an indoor hanging fern. At this point, Gina notices that her two hour mark is almost up and lets Wesley know that she's on a budget and satisfied with what they took today. Wesley tells her not to worry and that he's only charging her for the two hours no matter how long they take to finish all her shots. Gina is happy with this.

Gina doesn't hesitate to display her complete nakedness to Wesley as if they have known each other for multiple years. Wesley especially enjoys taking photos of Gina in yoga poses such as the Lotus position, Balasana or child pose, shavasana or corpse pose, Vrikshasana, Ustrasana, Sukhasana and supta baddha konasana. She does all of these poses with her eyes open in a few shots and then her eyes closed in another series of shots. (Wesley's suggestion.)

The last idea Gina has is to place rose petals in a tub of warm water. Wesley loves the idea and coaches Gina into various poses to match the tub with her thin body structure. He tests her limits on some of the poses because he wants to photograph her whole entire body. Gina shows no resistance in posing in every pose he suggests. Some of the poses Wesley suggests are scratching the borderline of artistic nude vs. very tame pornography.

Wesley's main strength, besides his photography skills, is his charm. He's the guy that can sell snow flakes to an Indigenous Alaskan in the wintertime. He finds ways to relate to his clients and makes them feel comfortable with him. He tells them stories about his life and is not afraid to share personal stories, even if they are hard to talk about. In turn, when he suggests to his clients some poses, the majority of the time, he can get his client to do the pose he wants even if they would say no to practically any other photographer. It's something about his age, his thin elderly Santa Claus look, white hair and the charisma in his voice that can get women to do almost any pose Wesley chooses.

After the photo shoot is done, Gina pays Wesley $250 dollars as they agreed upon on the phone. Wesley hands her back $100 dollars and says that since this is the last job of his long career, she can have $100 back. He also tells her that she can expect about 50 edited photos in about 3-4 days in her email. Gina tries to give back the $100, but

Wesley replies that he's very wealthy from wise stock and crypto currency investments over the years and doesn't need her money at all. He then gives back the other $150.

Wesley says, "Since you're my last professional client I'll ever have, this photo shoot is on me."

Gina asks, "Are you sure?"

Wesley replies, "I'm sure. Consider this a very early Christmas gift."

Gina, who's extremely happy, hugs Wesley and kisses him on the cheek.

"Mahalo. God bless you."

"God bless you too," Wesley says. He then adds, "Please don't tell anyone I gave you a free photo shoot. They might get jealous, especially your friend Jessica."

"Okay I won't."

Gina walks Wesley to the elevator and escorts him to his car in the visitors parking section. As Wesley is about to get into his car, he looks down on the ground and starts to cry. Gina asks if he's okay. Wesley tells her that he's technically been a professional photographer ever since he was 15 years old, so he's been doing this for 55 years. He also says that he's going to miss Hawai'i, since he leaves in four days to Washington State. Wesley tells Gina that he doesn't know if he will ever come back to Hawai'i. Gina wishes Wesley good luck in his retirement. Wesley composes himself and wishes a good life for Gina and her son Nalu. He drives away in a luxury rent a car.

Confrontation on the Beach

CHAPTER 5

While Gina was finishing up her photo shoot with Wesley, a smiling Jessica was at Lanikai Beach in Kailua. She was sunbathing with two of her former high school classmates, Amanda Crenshaw and Yuki Sato. All three graduated from Aiea High School together and were on the softball team. Ironically, Amanda and Yuki are certified nursing assistants at the same hospital Jessica and Gina work at, but on different floors. (Amanda works on a trauma floor and Yuki is on an orthopedic floor.)

Jessica just found out this morning that she's pregnant through an over the counter test. She texted Gina about the news, instead of calling her, because she knew she was probably in the middle of her photo shoot at the time Jessica took the test.

Amanda, who's African-American and Korean-American and 26 years of age, turns toward Jessica and asks her a question.

"Did you get a chance to tell your husband that you're pregnant?"

Jessica replies, "I emailed him a couple of hours ago, but he didn't respond. He's probably sleeping or on Mid-watch. It's about 3am where he is right now."

Yuki, who's also 26, says in a Hawaiian Creole Pidgin accent, "If your baby stay one girl, I get plenty baby clothes for you." (If your child is a girl, I have a lot of baby clothes for you.)

Jessica replies, "Mahalo Yuki. If it's a girl, I will take you up on your offer."

Amanda looks out towards the ocean at a couple of Caucasian men that obviously go to the gym. These men, in their early 20's, are body surfing in small waves that are gently crashing on the sand. Looking at their mannerisms and haircuts, they appear to be military, possibly Marine Corps.

Amanda turns toward her two friends.

"I don't know about you two, but I'm going over there to go swimming."

Yuki says, "I going join you soon, but I like get tiny bit more sun." (I will join you soon, I just want to sunbathe a little more.)

"Yuki, come on, there are two of them and two of us. Jessica doesn't count because she's married and now pregnant. We are both single. I'm going need a wing girl if I'm going talk to them." (Amanda sometimes switches over to a slight Pidgin English accent when speaking to Yuki, but generally speaks standard English or Ebonics to Jessica.)

Yuki sighs, "Okay, but I like talk to the one on the left. You can talk to the one on the right. The left one stay more handsome." (I would like to speak to the one of the left. You can speak to the one on the right. The one on the left is more handsome to me.)

Amanda says, "Yuki that's the one I wanted to speak to... Okay then, let's jan ken po (Rock, paper, scissors.)"

Amanda and Yuki participate in jan ken po for three rounds. In the end, Amanda shows paper and Yuki shows rock.

Amanda says with a huge smile, "I win."

Dejected, Yuki exclaims, "Ah crap."

Jessica watches her two friends confidently walk over to the two men in the surf. Amanda is 5' 8", an inch taller than both Jessica and

Gina. She's wearing a lime green two piece G-string bikini and is more muscular than the average woman because she works out in the gym. Yuki is 5' 2", and is wearing a blue bikini top and grey female surf shorts. Both Amanda and Yuki are skinny and attractive women who both recently got out of bad relationships.

A year ago, Amanda started dating an African-American man originally from San Francisco, California. At first, things were good, but after a few months, they got into big arguments over his excessive drinking. Amanda tried to convince him to go into rehab, but the man didn't want help. After a couple of arguments and no signs of the man wanting to seek help, Amanda broke it off. The man decided that Hawai'i wasn't working out and moved back to the Bay Area.

Yuki, who's mainly Japanese, but has a small amount of Chinese and Korean, started dating a Caucasian man, from Hawai'i Island, about six months ago. At first, their relationship was good, except for the fact that the guy didn't really get along with Yuki's three year old daughter Mia. (Mia's father, who passed away two years ago from an aneurysm, was half-Puerto Rican, half-Mexican. He died at the age of 25.)

Yuki noticed that the guy didn't really want to interact with Mia and barely acknowledged her when they were in the same room together. The man originally talked about wanting children someday, but after discussions with him about how he wasn't interacting with Mia that often, the man admitted that he probably didn't want to have children and that they should break up. Yuki was sad in one way and relieved in another. She felt that if the man didn't want children in his future and she did, then this man wasn't the one for her. Plus, if he wasn't to interact with her daughter, that was another huge red flag and a sign to move on from him.

Amanda and Yuki start talking to the two men, who are about 40 yards away from Jessica. Jessica obviously can't hear the conversation, but through body language, they seem friendly. However, Jessica can tell that they are not interested in flirting with her two friends. Jessica wonders if the two men are a couple. She then has a thought about a first cousin of hers on Kaua'i, who is married to another man and has an adopted five-year old foster daughter. Jessica realizes that she hasn't texted or spoken to him for a few months now and should call him sometime to see how he's doing.

About 30 seconds later, Jessica notices a Caucasian woman and an African-American woman briskly walking down the beach towards Amanda, Yuki and the two men. Both women are in their early 20's and recently moved to Hawai'i from California. The two women exchange negative words with Amanda and Yuki and embrace the two men. The Caucasian woman passionately kisses one of the men, making it clear that this man is off limits. (The man she kisses is the one Amanda and Yuki were not interested in as much as the other man.)

Amanda and the Caucasian woman exchange more words. Some of them are swear words like bitch and other stronger words. Jessica can hear Amanda's Ebonics coming out and knows that Amanda has a black belt in Brazilian Ju-jitsu and Yuki has a brown belt in Judo. Jessica knows that both girls can fight, especially Amanda who has a record of 7-0-1 in tournaments here in Hawai'i. A couple of Professional mixed martial arts organizations in Asia and the United States have contacted Amanda and told her that they will be watching her next fight to decide if they will recruit her in the future. Potential deals could be worth hundreds of thousands of dollars.

Yuki holds back Amanda, who wants to fight the Caucasian woman. The Caucasian woman is taunting Amanda in Ebonics. This woman is really skinny and by her looks, doesn't seem like she can fight, although looks can sometimes be deceiving. The two European-American men firmly ask both Amanda and Yuki to leave their group alone and go somewhere else. Amanda loses her mind and wants to fight both men. Yuki holds her back.

Jessica stands up and starts walking over to help break things up or back up her friends. (When Jessica was at Aiea High School, she got into her fair share of fights and is not afraid to mix it up with women or even men.) While Jessica was preparing to either help break this situation up or help back up her friends, she remembers she's pregnant and shouldn't jeopardize the baby inside her. Jessica whistles loudly and gets the attention of the whole beach, which is crowded.

Jessica yells in Hawaiian Creole Pidgin English, "Eh, never mind those guys! They nothing! Worry about your MMA fight!" (Don't worry about them, worry about your MMA fight coming up!)

Amanda exchanges swear words with the European-American men and shows them the finger. Amanda and Yuki then walk about 150 yards in a different direction and go swimming. At that moment, Jessica's phone rings. She sees that it's Gina.

"Hello."

"Hey pregnant lady," says a smiling Gina on her cell-phone.

"I'm so happy. It's such an amazing feeling." Jessica replies.

"It is and I'll be here to help you every step of the way, but I better be named your child's Godmother," says Gina in a half-jokingly manner.

"Of course you will. Franklin and I were starting to get doubts if we were ever going to be pregnant. We were looking at IUI and IVF, even though we are both only in our 20's."

Gina says, "Well you don't have to look at those options now."

"Thanks to God," exclaims Jessica.

Gina asks, "So did you tell your husband that you're pregnant yet?"

"I emailed him the news, but he didn't respond yet. In addition, I emailed him the evening gown photos only. I decided that's the only photos I want him to see. I hid the rest of the photos deep in my computer. So it looks like you and I are the only ones that know those photos exist."

"Okay," says Gina nonchalantly.

Jessica tells Gina about the near fight Amanda, Yuki and a group of people almost got into. After listening to the story, Gina says that Amanda and Yuki would of kicked those girls asses and possibly even the two guys. Gina reminds Jessica that Amanda has to train with men only in her MMA gym because there are currently no women in that gym that can come close to her level.

"Amanda can hold her own against men," adds Gina.

Jessica says, "I was more worried about her thin bikini being ripped off. You know how she likes to go practically naked at the beach sometimes."

Gina starts to chuckle. She then asks, "Is she wearing that lime green G-stringed bikini today?"

"Yes."

"The one we tell her is slightly see-through when wet, but she doesn't seem to care?"

Jessica, laughing, says, "Yes that one."

Gina starts to laugh. She then changes the subject and proceeds to tell Jessica about her photo shoot and how she felt Wesley was a true gentlemen. She was really impressed by his professionalism. Jessica asks what type of poses she did. Gina answers her questions and is anxious to show Jessica the photos. Gina didn't tell her that she got the photo shoot for free, because she doesn't want to make Jessica jealous. Jessica is excited for her.

"When you get your photos, I want to see them. Well the ones that will not scar me for life," Jessica says jokingly.

Gina laughs. "No worries, I'll show you the ones that are not pornographic." Jessica, caught off guard, asks, "What?"

The Deception

CHAPTER 6

Two weeks ago, Wesley Smith sold his luxuriously four bedroom beach front home in Waikīkī to a Mainland investor who's going to turn the property into a vacation rental. For a brief moment, Wesley had slight reservations in selling his home to a very rich Mainland investor, who's known to turn beachfront homes into vacation rentals. Wesley's lived in Hawai'i for half a century and knows the struggles Hawai'i residents have in finding housing. Many residents are forced to move to the US Mainland to buy homes that are much more affordable. They leave the islands they love, which still have some resemblance of the Aloha Spirit left, and trade it in for a generally harsher, less friendly, more cut throat, survival of the fittest style of living in the US Mainland.

Hawai'i can be a hard place to live if you don't own a home, apartment or have an affordable place to stay. Shipping companies charge high premiums on goods coming into the docks. (They usually do this with the full backing of Hawai'i politicians.) This makes products shipped into Hawai'i so much more expensive than in the US Mainland.

Jobs, while they are around, are sometimes competitive in many fields that pay good money. Illegal drugs are sadly here and crime, unfortunately is here too. If Hawai'i didn't have a great melting pot and the Aloha Spirit, (here and there), many Hawai'i residents would bail out on this paradise in droves.

Wesley looked at bids for his home with his real estate agent and went with the highest bidder that offered cash. He was really sad to let go of his three female renters last month. He thought of them as more than just tenants and especially liked that they all paid on time. For the last two weeks, after selling his home and car, Wesley has stayed in a upscale hotel in Waikīkī. He remembers the good times he had in Hawai'i, but feels it's time to be close to his family on the Mainland.

Wesley tried his hand at marriage and was successful at it. He had two sons with his longtime wife of 40 years that he met in church. Unfortunately, she died five years ago from lung cancer and that's when his whole life started to spiral downward spiritually. He started cursing God and stopped going to church. A former God fearing Christian, Wesley did a 180 degree turn and now blames God for his wife's death. (Not her cigarette smoking.) While Wesley still believes in God, Wesley's anger towards Him has consumed Wesley and made his honor code change from caring about others to becoming selfish and only caring about himself, his family and most importantly to him, his wealth.

Most people see death as something that will happen to all of us and generally accept it as part of the circle of life, while others seek someone to blame when things don't go their way. Some people choose to blame God for bad things that happen to them or their loved ones, even though God is the one that gave the gift of life to all of us in the first place. (Without God, we would have never taken our first breath and experienced this world for what it has to offer, both the good and the bad.)

Before Wesley went to his going away party his friend Philip was throwing for him, at Philip's home in Mānoa, Wesley turned on his laptop. He looked over all his different investment portfolios. Overall, he calculated that if he liquidated all his stocks, crypto currencies, real estate and cash investments in his various accounts, he would have over 10 million dollars.

Looking at the way he dresses and how he carries himself, you wouldn't think he's worth 10 million dollars. He dresses in Aloha shirts, shorts and slippers pretty much everyday of his life. Wesley through both luck and wise thinking, took a huge chance and invested $10,000 dollars in the right stocks and crypto currencies when their value was low and now reaps the rewards that these investments are paying out like an out of control slot machine.

Wesley happily enters Philip's home for his going away party. About three dozen friends have gathered to say goodbye. Half of the guests are of European-American ancestry and the other half are either Asian, mixed-Asian, Caucasian/Asian or mixed Polynesian. To no ones surprise, most of the guests are female and a good majority are in their 40-50's. Most of these females have been photographed by Wesley at least once.

At first, Philip, who's half Caucasian, half Asian and 49 years of age, proposed a "pot luck." A pot luck is an old tradition in Hawai'i where every guest or guest family unit brings a main dish or desert. A few people bring drinks like beer or soda, while a tiny percentage might bring a bag of chips, paper plates, forks, a bag of ice or napkins. The freeloaders, which are usually rare, just bring themselves. (These freeloaders tend to be not familiar with Hawai'i customs, cheapskates or just aren't aware an event was a potluck.)

Wesley told everyone that while, "he loves eating exotic foods from different ethnicities," he wanted to go out in style. Wesley hired one of his Japanese friends, a renown Sushi chef originally from Tokyo, to cater his party using his five star restaurant. The guests were beyond impressed with his fresh sushi and other Japanese delicacies he made. (Wesley made sure to tip his friend well.)

Throughout the night, people say their goodbyes to Wesley. Some even make him cry.

Wesley must have been in over two hundred photos or selfies and could easily have been in a hundred more. Wesley's whole life is photography, so taking and being in photos is something he could do blindfolded or in his sleep.

As his guests leave one by one or in small groups, Wesley urges them to take home leftovers in take out containers. Neither Wesley or Philip want to deal with leftovers. (Besides, taking leftovers from a party, in Hawai'i, is a tradition that dates back from long ago.)

After Wesley says goodbye to his last guest, his all night smile turns into a business demeanor. Wesley grabs his lap top from his backpack and sits down next to Philip at a dinner table. He logs into a Dark Web account, then shows Philip a large amount of photos. Philip looks through about 300 photos from about a dozen Hawai'i women Wesley took over the last month. These women are of various ethnicities. Most of the photos are implied nudes, semi-nudes or artistic nudes, but a few are photos Wesley took in secret while his clients were not paying attention. Wesley has a camera that can snap photos without making a sound. He also presses record on his camera and later takes still shots from video. Most of the women in the photos are in their 30-40's, but there are a few in their 20's.

Philip is impressed with Jessica Cromwell-Tanner's photos.

"Oh I love this one, she has a nice pussy."

Wesley smiles and says, "Funny story. She didn't want me to take a photo of her vagina, but I recorded video in between takes and took screenshots off of the video. I couldn't let such a nice pussy get away from my camera. Plus I know what type of shots you like best, so I tailor some of the shots just for your liking."

"Thank you Gerald. I feel honored."

Philip looks through Jessica's batch of photos and loves it over the other women that Wesley shot. Philip really likes her shower photos. Wesley provides Philip with more shots of her vaginal area while she was in the shower.

Philip says, "I wish I could meet this woman. She's so beautiful."

Wesley smiles. "You think you love this woman, wait till you see the next one. Get ready to be amazed my friend."

Wesley shows Philip the photos of Gina Grey. He starts off showing him a few of her non-nude hula shots, then her implied and artistic nudes. These photos really capture Philip's imagination, but it's the nude yoga poses that really blow Philip away.

"Oh my God. Out of all the women you have showed me over the last four years, this woman is absolutely the best."

"I know, she may not be the most beautiful woman I've ever photographed, but she's the most natural at posing," says Wesley.

"I agree."

Wesley clicks on a folder. It opens, revealing two dozen photos of Gina in the bathtub with rose petals around her.

Wesley says, "A few of these photos came out slightly pornographic in nature, so I know you will love them."

Philip looks at the photos and is absolutely stunned.

"Oh my…what is this? This is mind-blowing."

Philip is practically salivating looking at these photos of Gina.

"Is that all the photos from this batch of women?"

Wesley replies, "Yes it is."

"I want them all. How much?"

"Well Philip, since you have been my most consistent and loyal customer buying these type of photos from me over the last four years, I'm going to sell them all to you for 1/2 the price you usually pay. How's that?"

"Wow really? Oh my God yes!" Wesley smiles.

Philip asks, "Hey did you get those other pictures I requested from your friend in Asia?"

"Yes I did. Thanks for reminding me. I forgot about those. My memory is not like it used to be when I was in my youth."

Wesley goes onto a Dark Web site and starts typing for about two minutes to retrieve and open up an encrypted file.

"You and I will be seeing this for the first time."

Wesley opens the file. It's dozens of photos of underage Southeast Asian girls without clothing.

Wesley turns away from the screen and says, "I can't look at this."

Philip looks at the photos. He asks if this batch is the usual price.

Wesley closes the file and says, "Since this is the last time we will be doing business together, and I'm disgusted by these photos, I'll give them to you at half your usual price as well. Just pay for all the photos you purchased tonight in Bitcoin or Etherium."

"I have Bitcoin."

"And I love Bitcoin. You know that," says Wesley.

Philip goes to one of his crypto currency accounts and transfers Bitcoin to Wesley. Once Wesley sees that the Bitcoin is in his account, Wesley transfers all the photos to Philip's encrypted Dark Web account.

Wesley says, "Mahalo Philip for all your business."

Philip replies, "It's my pleasure Gerald. Thank you for supplying great photos to me over the years."

Wesley shakes hands with his friend. Philip asks an important question.

"Why do you tell people your name is Wesley Smith, when your name is really Gerald Williams?"

"Wesley Smith is my professional name. Like how a few actors or writers use a pen name that is made up, I did the same. And besides, I have to have a fake name when selling these type of photos to someone like you."

Philip laughs. Wesley also laughs. They exchange small talk before Wesley gets a text on his cell-phone from his European-American girlfriend.

"My girlfriend's texting me," says Wesley.

Wesley reads the text, which says, "Are you ready to get picked up?"

Wesley texts back, "Sure, please come now."

He gets back a text from her that reads, "Okay."

Philip asks, "How old is your girlfriend?"

"38," replies Wesley.

Philip's caught off guard with her age.

"Wow. You're 70 and she's 38. How do you do it?"

"I ain't going to lie to you Philip. Money talks. There are a lot of rich older men with young girlfriends or wives. My girlfriend knows I have money, so that's why she's with me. I found her on a website that features younger women looking for sugar daddies."

Philip laughs for a moment, then asks, "Do you have a photo of her?"

"I do."

Wesley shows him a picture of his girlfriend on his phone. She is very attractive. Philip immediately recognizes her from a batch of nude photos he bought tonight and a previous batch of nude photos from last month.

Philip blatantly asks, "Does she know that you sold nude photos of her to me?"

Wesley replies, "No she has no clue and I doubt she will ever find out."

Philip asks, "Are you taking her to Washington State with you in a few days?"

"Hell no. I've only started dating her four months ago. She's begging me to take her, but I can't do it. She's too much of a gold digger and costing me too much. Plus if I take her, I have to take her 16 year-old daughter who's a meth addict. The girl's already been caught twice stealing money out of her mom's purse. I don't want to deal with her stealing or addiction. I'm also tired of my girlfriend constantly wanting me to buy her expensive bags, dresses and jewelry. And when she wants something, she doesn't ask nicely, she blatantly says, 'buy me that bag or buy me that diamond necklace.' What is that all about? At least ask in a polite way and say please and thank you. She never says please or thank you. It's as if she feels entitled to it."

"Man, I wouldn't want to deal with a woman like that or with a drug addict daughter that likes to steal. If the girl stole stuff from me, I'm going to do something to her that's going to land me in jail."

"I understand. Besides her 16 year-old with sticky fingers, she has a 21 year-old son and a 19 year-old son. The 21 year-old just started a ten-year sentence in a Federal Prison in Arizona for Meth and Heroin distribution. Her 19 year-old is the only smart one of the three. He joined the Army and is getting trained as a truck mechanic in Germany. He called the mom yesterday and said he has a Vietnamese girlfriend that speaks fluent German and was actually born there."

Philip says, "That's interesting…If you took your girlfriend to Washington State, your sons, who are older than her, might wonder why you are dating her."

"That's right. My oldest is 45 and youngest is 41. Imagine if I married this woman, they would have a step-mom that is younger than both of them."

Both Wesley and Philip start to laugh. They engage in more small talk until the girlfriend arrives to picks Wesley up. Wesley hugs Philip before he goes in the car.

Philip doesn't get to meet his girlfriend, but sees her from his window. Wesley waves goodbye to Philip as he drives off. Wesley sheds a couple of tears because he viewed Philip as a friend and not only a client he sold nude photos to for the last four years.

As Wesley is being driven to his hotel room in Waikīkī, he feels a little guilty that he mislead Philip about his true name and destination that he's going to. He told most people that his name was Wesley Smith and only about a half-dozen people that his name was really Gerald Williams. That is a lie. His actual real name is John Jones. He also told everyone, in Hawai'i, that he's going to Washington State to retire, but in reality, he's really going to Upstate New York. The only honest thing he told people in Hawai'i was about is his family. (His wife dying five years ago from lung cancer and that he has two sons and five grandchildren.)

Wesley starts thinking about three local photographers he made strong friendships with here in Hawai'i. (Two of them are men and the third is a woman.) All three of them had paid gigs tonight, so they could not attend the party. Whenever Wesley met with these three, usually on an individual basis, they would share with each other photos of women they took as if they were trading cards or trophies. This included nude photos of women they photographed.

    Wesley loved looking at nude photos of females that his friends took, but especially liked showing off his photos to them because he felt his photographic skills were so much more dominate than his friends. Wesley always wanted to be the best in anything he did.

More Photo Sharing

CHAPTER 7

On the day Wesley left for New York, Gina received 50 professionally edited photos in her email. Gina texted Jessica and told her about them. After her overnight shift at the hospital ended at 7:30am, Jessica went home and showered. She then went to Gina's house and looked at all the photos. Jessica especially loved Gina's rose petal photo series. Gina loved them too, but didn't show Jessica the borderline pornographic photos and other photos that show her private area clearly.

Jessica said, "These photos are really beautiful."

Gina replies, "I know. Wesley sure knows his stuff. He's the best photographer I ever met."

"I agree. Hey are you planning on showing anyone else these photos?"

"I'll show the non-nudes, like the hula ones to people and put it on social media, but all the other photos, you and I will be the only ones that will ever see these photos, unless I show them to a future husband."

"Same with my (nude) photos. I know my husband couldn't handle seeing them if he knew a man took them. And I don't want to lie to him about who took the photos. I could easily say a woman took them and he would probably be okay with that."

Gina says, "Would he still get mad if he knew that Wesley was a harmless 70 year-old man that looks like a skinny Santa Claus?"

"I don't want to take the chance. I'll just keep them for myself to look at every once in a blue moon."

"Okay...Hey do you want to come with me to pick up my son at my ex-mother in-laws apartment? Since I have the next three days off, it's my turn to spend time with Nalu."

"Sure. Why not?"

Gina and Jessica drive out to pick up Gina's son in a city called Makiki. After they pick him up, they go out and eat at an organic foods restaurant.

A few days later, a 28 year-old Far East Asian man, named Terrence, visits his former co-worker Philip, at Philip's home. Philip and Terrence used to work together as security guards in a hotel in Waikīkī. Last year, Terrence was forced to resign because he was caught sleeping on the job for the third time in a two month period. (And he couldn't deny it because he was sleeping at the main desk with a known camera right in front of him.) The first two times, he was written up. A few months after being forced to resign, Terrence got a job as a transporter in the same hospital Jessica and Gina work at.

For over a month now, Philip has been selling Terrence photos of nude women he obtained from Wesley. Philip doesn't mind selling his friend these types of photos because he does it on the Dark Web on a secure site anyway. Money is money to Philip. The only photos Philip doesn't show Terrence is his large child pornography collection. Philip sells these photos on a very secretive, encrypted Dark Web site and has never told a soul about them in person.

Terrence shifts through the 300 or so photos Philip bought last week and notices a Chinese/Caucasian woman that he went to high school with. He immediately asks to buy those photos for $25. Philip says okay to the price since there are ten photos in this set. Terrence then sees Jessica and Gina and is very surprised to see them.

Terrence says, "OMG, I can't believe Jessica and Gina took nude photos with your friend. They are nurses at the hospital I work at. I see them from time to time. They both work the night shift on a heart (cardiac) floor."

Philip replies, "Nurses huh? Maybe they can give me a sponge bath."

Both Philip and Terrence laugh.

After Terrence is done laughing, he asks Philip how much for all of the pictures of both women. Philip says he can give it to him for $300, since there are 50 photos in both set. Terrence picks out 20 photos out of Gina's set and 15 photos out of Jessica's set and negotiates $100 photos for 35 photos. Terrence keeps on looking through the rest of the photos and ends up spending $75 more in photos of various Hawai'i women. Philip is happy because he ends up making $175 off of Terrence that day.

Philip realizes Terrence could easily pick nude photos off the internet for free; however, the high quality of shots helps draw people like Terrence and others to buy photos shot by Wesley through Philip.

The next day, Terrence goes into work and immediately seeks out a couple of male transporters he feels he can trust. In the transporter break room, he shows them his set of nude photos of Jessica, Gina and several other Hawai'i women. The transporters, a Caucasian guy named Jerry and a Hispanic/Asian guy named Richard, both in their 20's, are practically speechless.

Terrence makes a deal and sells the photos of Jessica, Gina and other women for $50 each. Terrence texts them the photos to their phones. Throughout the day, Terrence, Jerry and Richard go around and show the photos of Jessica and Gina to other people they know in the hospital.

With people they trust, Terrence and Jerry makes deals and sells off nude photos of the two nurses. (Whatever they can get.) Richard shows the photos to others and text them freely to his friends. This goes on and on and starts to snowball over the next two weeks. Terrence ends up pocketing $400 from sales and Jerry $150. The three guys text the photos to some of their co-workers and in turn, these co-workers text the nude photos to others they know and feel would be interested in seeing them.

Jessica and Gina are not aware that their nude photos are being texted around the hospital freely or sold off to co-workers. Most of the people seeing the photos are males, but a few are females. Occasionally, both Jessica and Gina get little stares or giggles that they notice, but have no clue why.

Photos around the World

CHAPTER 8

After two weeks of people showing off and texting Jessica and Gina's photos throughout the hospital, one of her friends finds out about it. While getting ready to go to bed, Amanda Crenshaw receives a text from her 25 year-old African-American female cousin named Denisha Crenshaw.

Denisha is a nurse at the same hospital as Amanda, Jessica, Gina and Yuki. The text has two completely nude photos of Jessica in the shower and two nude photos of Gina in the bath tube with rose petals. The caption says, "OMG. Look at these two naked bitches. Lol." Amanda, not happy, texts her cousin back and writes, "Those two naked bitches are my friends!!!!! Not funny!!!!!"

Upset, Amanda immediately calls her cousin. Denisha is apologetic and says she didn't know that they were Amanda's friends. Amanda doesn't care about an apology. She just wants to know where Denisha got the photos. Denisha, now scared, told her that she got them for free from a male transporter named Jerry, who bought them from a transporter named Terrence. Amanda is livid. She further questions her cousin and finds out that Terrence and Jerry have been showing and selling people nude photos of Jessica and Gina for about two weeks now.

Furious, Amanda says, "I can't believe this is happening to my friends. I'm going to get to the bottom of this and kick Terrence and Jerry's asses."

Amanda's cousin advises her not to kick anyone's ass because it could jeopardize her upcoming MMA fight in two months. In turn, that could mess up her chances of getting into an MMA pro league in Asia or the US. Amanda agrees. Denisha then asks Amanda to keep her name out of this. Amanda assures her that she will keep her name out of this as best as she can. This is not a good enough assurance to Denisha, who tells her that she's the one that brought it to Amanda's attention. Amanda says she will do her best to keep Denisha autonomous.

Denisha alerts Amanda that besides the photos being circulated through the hospital, Jessica and Gina have nude photos on various sites on the internet.

Amanda asks, "What sites?!"

Denisha replies, "They are on a Hawai'i women nude site and a couple of girlfriend revenge type of sites."

"Can you screen shot the sites and get me the URL's, so I can help Jessica and Gina take down their photos off any sites they are on."

"Okay I will," says Denisha."

Amanda asks how Denisha found out about the websites her friends are on. Her cousin says that Jerry told her about it and showed her at work. Denisha again says she's sorry about sending the nude photos and will give Amanda the URL's and screenshots as soon as possible.

After hanging up the phone, Amanda takes a deep breath and doesn't know what to do next. This news is overwhelming her because she has taken nude photos in the past and would be very upset if her photos were made public and shown around her workplace or put on the internet. An angry Amanda calls her best friend Yuki.

When Yuki hears the story, she's shocked that Terrence and Jerry are sharing or selling nude photos of her two friends. In a high pitched Hawaiian Creole Pidgin English accent, she immediately says that they need to go speak to Jessica and Gina and then need to go to their supervisor and human resources to find a way to stop people from showing and spreading their photos. They also need to question Terrence on where he originally got these photos he sold to Jerry. In addition, Yuki says that they need to find a way to get Jessica and Gina's nude photos off those internet sites her cousin Denisha spoke about.

Right on cue, Denisha sends three screenshots and URL's to Amanda.

Amanda says, "My cousin just sent me URL's and screenshots of the sites."

"Check them out, I'll stay on the line," says Yuki.

Amanda types up the first URL and sees several nude photos of Jessica and Gina on a site featuring women from Hawai'i.

Amanda is disgusted to see that her friends nude photos are posted here without permission. The other two sites with Jessica and Gina's nude photos are revenge sites. Amanda tells Yuki that she will contact Jessica and Gina now.

After Amanda gets off the phone with Yuki, she texts Jessica and Gina and asks them to call her. (Amanda knew they were both at work on the night shift.) When Jessica calls back, Amanda tells Jessica that both Jessica and Gina have nude photos circulating around the hospital and on at least three internet sites. Jessica freaks out. She motions for Gina to come over. Jessica and Gina go to a quiet conference room and put the phone on speaker. Amanda quietly tells Jessica and Gina the horrible news about Terrance and Jerry selling and spreading their nude photos around the hospital. She tells them about the websites and sends them the four photos her cousin Denisha sent her. She also sends the URL links. Both girls check out the photos and links and are shocked.

"F##K!" Gina yells.

Jessica exclaims, "F##king Wesley must of sold Terrence and Jerry nude photos of us! And either Terrence, Jerry or someone else posted it on those sites! Unless Wesley posted our photos!?"

Gina exclaims, "I don't f##king know! This is crazy!"

Gina clinches her hair with both her hands. She starts to cry. Jessica starts crying as well.

A couple of co-workers look towards the conference room. They hear Jessica and Gina yelling, but don't say anything because they know they must be speaking about the nude photos of themselves.

Amanda says, "I'm sorry I had to bring this bad news to you, but I felt I needed to."

"You did the right thing. Thank you for letting us know," says Jessica.

"Gina adds, "Mahalo for calling us. Let us take it from here."

Before Amanda gets off the phone, she says that Yuki suggested they speak to Seo-Yeon and human resources and find a way to take down the photos off those websites.

Gina says, "Those are good ideas. I"ll make sure to thank Yuki for the advice."

Amanda says her goodbyes and hangs up the phone. Jessica looks at Gina and apologizes. She starts crying.

"I'm sorry I got you involved in this mess by bringing Wesley into our lives."

Gina paces the floor before saying, "It isn't your fault. It's Wesley's fault. Wesley obviously screwed us and released our nude photos into the world without our permission. He must of sold the photos to Terrence and Jerry."

Jessica says, "He did. He betrayed us...I hope my husband doesn't find out about the photos."

Gina sighs, then says, "You might want to tell him. If he finds out before you say something, that could be very bad. And he's bound to find out sooner or later."

Jessica sighs, "You're absolutely right. I have to tell him, but I don't know how or when...I wonder how many people have seen these photos here in the hospital and on those sites?"

"I don't know, but now we know why some of our co-workers have been looking at us and giggling."

Gina decides to call Wesley to see why he sold the photos without their permission. She gets a disconnected phone message.

Gina sighs again. "That a##hole disconnected his phone! I can't believe Santa Claus deceived us!"

"F##k," exclaims Jessica.

Gina looks at Jessica and says, "We should take Yuki's advice and speak to our manager (Seo-Yeon) and human resources about this matter. We can't have our nude photos circulating throughout the hospital. This hospital has thousands of workers. And we have to figure out how to get our naked photos off those websites."

Jessica, crying, asks Gina if she can go home early. Since Gina is the charge nurse of the floor tonight and the floor is slow with a couple of empty beds, Gina says she can go home after she finishes passing her midnight medications and charting.

The registered nurses and nursing assistances on the floor feel sorry for Jessica and Gina. All of them heard the rumor of the existence of their nude photos circulating around the hospital, but didn't say a word to inform Jessica or Gina. Jessica finishes passing her medications and completes all her charting. She goes home a little after 2am. Gina takes over her five patients. Previously, Gina had zero as the charge nurse.

The next morning, after her shift is done at 730am, Gina goes to Seo-Yeon and tells her what's going on. Seo-Yeon, a Korean-American woman in her late 50's, used to work with Gina and Jessica on the floor until she became the manager last year. She absorbs what Gina says and is in shock for a moment. She then becomes visibly angry.

Seo-Yeon makes a phone call to human resources and lets them know what's going on. An HR manager says that what Terrence and Jerry allegedly did is considered sexual harassment under company rules and that if Terrence and Jerry did indeed sell and show off nude photos of Jessica and Gina, then they are subject to being terminated. HR also said to Seo-Yeon that they will have to start an investigation immediately.

Gina says that she will have to get the police involved because a photographer illegally sold or gave Terrence the nude photos he sold to Jerry. Seo-Yeon says to Gina that she will speak to her Detective friend named Lopaka Kameda at the Honolulu Police Department on Beretania Street. Seo-Yeon tells Gina to go home and get some rest since HR is going to do an investigation and handle Terrence and Jerry internally.

Gina goes home very angry. After taking a shower, she feels exhausted and goes to sleep. While she is sleeping, human resources calls Terrence and Jerry and asks them to come in at noon, three hours before they are scheduled to work. Both Terrence and Jerry come in with tears in their eyes. They both know they screwed up big time.

In the hearing, conducted at human resources, Terrence and Jerry had two female union representatives representing them and protecting their rights. HR had three representatives. The first person was a middle-aged, Caucasian female HR representative. The second person was a 38 year-old hospital lawyer named Clarence Sato, (Yuki Sato's uncle) and the third was Seo-Yeon.

After some heavy questioning, Terrence and Jerry both made full confessions and apologized.

Terrence went further and said he bought photos from a guy he knew, but had no clue where he got the photos from. Terrence and Jerry both said they had no grudges against Jessica and Gina and didn't know them personally. HR said they were placing Terrence and Jerry under suspension without pay pending further investigation. The union representatives jumped in and made sure that Terrence and Jerry were allowed to use vacation time to financially cover their days of suspension. That was reluctantly accepted.

Terrence and Jerry both agreed to write down the names of everyone at work they either sold or showed the nude photos of Jessica and Gina in exchange for special considerations later on. Both men were crying and remorseful.

Over the next two weeks, human resources brought in everyone on Terrence and Jerry's list to speak to them. If they were found to have purchased the nude photos, they were suspended for two weeks and asked to delete the photos off their phone in front of human resources. If they freely passed on the photo through texts, they were suspended for a week and had to delete the photos in front of HR. If they were caught selling the photos, they would be terminated.

Most people denied involvement. Only one person confessed to seeing the photos, but said it was only in passing outside the hospital grounds and they didn't even know it was Gina and Jessica. (The man said that if he knew it was of two employees, he would have told HR himself.)

After days of discussions between multiple unions and the hospital, it was determined that only Terrence and Jerry would be punished, since the unions for 10 people named were threatening serious grievances if anyone other than Terrence and Jerry were held responsible. Both Terrence and Jerry were terminated, but were allowed to cash in any accumulated vacation time.

HR gave a verbal (undocumented) warning to anyone who was named by Terrence or Jerry. They were warned that they would face termination if they share or sell any nude photos of Gina or Jessica going forward. Some of the people who actually saw the photos included: nurses; nurse aides; transporters; respiratory techs; ward clerks; radiation techs; x-ray techs; physical therapists; occupational therapists; food service workers; housekeepers; security guards; IT workers; parking lot attendants; maintenance workers and a few other occupations. (No one wanted to share the photos with any doctors because they felt that a doctor would feel obligated to turn them in.)

In all, over 500 workers and some of their family members viewed or passed on Jessica and Gina's nude photos, however, only 10 were brought into HR. When Gina and Jessica found out the final results that only Terrence and Jerry were terminated and the others only received verbal warnings, they were beyond livid. They both told HR that the number 10 has to be a very low number compared to who really saw the photos.

The Detective, Lawyer and Real Photographer

CHAPTER 9

After Gina woke up from her sleep the morning she found out about the nude photos at work and on the internet, she calls the Honolulu Police Department. She asks to speak to Detective Lopaka Kameda. Detective Kameda listens to Gina's complaint and asks if she signed a contract with Wesley. Gina told him that Jessica and herself signed a 14 page contract. Kameda asks if she could come down to the station and show him both contracts.

Two hours later, Jessica and Gina arrive at the Police Station on Beretania Street and meet with Detective Kameda. Detective Kameda, a 55 year-old Japanese, Portuguese and Hawaiian man, with salt and pepper hair, looks over the contract.

Speaking with a slight Hawaiian Creole Pidgin English accent, Detective Kameda says, "Ladies, this contract is confusing, but it's a model release contract. You are the fourth and fifth woman to come in here in the last week with the same exact contract from Mr. Smith. Sadly, this contract gives Mr. Smith legal permission to use your photos however he wants to, including selling them. It's a very confusing contract, but it basically says that he retains 100% right over your photos and can do what he wants with them."

Jessica says, "Oh my goodness. So we can't file criminal charges against Wesley Smith or get our photos down off of internet sites?"

Detective Kameda replies, "I never said that, but it's going to be a little harder than usual to go after Mr. Smith for criminal charges with this type of contract. However, since Mr. Smith appears to have misled the both of you, you may be able to challenge the contract legality in court. And to me, it appears that a good lawyer could argue that Mr. Smith grossly misled you."

Gina says, "I wanted to get my glasses when he presented the contract to me, but he said for me not to worry about what it says because all it said was I give him money and he would give me photos."

"A good lawyer might be able to get your contract voided, but I'm not a lawyer. I want you two to go see my good friend Clarence Sato. He's a lawyer and him and I went to Maui High School together."

Gina says, "Okay."

Detective Kameda writes down Clarence Sato's number twice and gives it to Gina and Jessica. The two women thank the detective for the number.

Kameda says, "Sato will also be able to advise you on legal matters concerning this incident. Let him know I sent you and to have him call me right after you speak to him. Also, please give me the URL's or the site name that has your photos. I'll see what my IT guy can do concerning figuring out who posted your photos."

Gina and Jessica give Detective Kameda the information. They then thank him for his help. They leave feeling mixed feelings of hope and despair.

After they get into Gina's car, Gina says, "Clarence Sato? He wants us to talk to him? Every time we fight for more pay or benefits in nursing contract negotiations, Sato's always fighting hard for the hospital. I know he's Yuki's uncle, but I hate talking to Sato. He's just so committed to saving every little penny for the hospital, it's sickening."

Jessica replies, "And that's exactly why we want him to fight for us and help us in this situation. If he's on our side fighting for us, then we are in good hands."

Gina pauses for a moment, then realizes Jessica's right. Just on cue, Gina gets a phone call from the hospital. It's Clarence Sato. Sato says he wants to speak to Gina and Jessica in his Downtown office. Gina speaks to Jessica briefly, then sets up a meeting with him an hour from now. Gina briefly tells her about Mr. Smith and the whole story that lead them to this moment, including the internet sites.

Sato is taken aback by what he hears. He then asks Gina if it would be okay for his fiancé to be in the meeting to help shed some light on this situation. Both Jessica and Gina say that it would be okay.

Jessica and Gina, who were given the next two days off with pay because of the circumstances, go to Mr. Sato's office in Downtown Honolulu. Sato's secretary shows them to a back meeting room and offers them water or coffee. Jessica and Gina both ask for water. Shortly after receiving the water, Sato's 34 year-old fiancé, named Amelia Espanto, walks into the room wearing a Navy blue professional dress. Espanto is primarily Filipina, but has a little bit of Spanish and Chinese ancestry. She once took a couple of prerequisite classes for nursing at the University of Hawai'i with Gina and Jessica before changing course and becoming a social worker instead. Gina and Jessica both remember her and exchange pleasantries. Espanto lets them know that besides being a social worker, she's also a part-time photographer on the weekends and can offer incite on what they are going through.

After a little small talk, Sato walks into the room wearing a professional grey suit. He greets both women.

Gina says, "I'm not used to seeing you if it's not nursing contract negotiations or in a family picture Yuki shows me."

Sato, Jessica and Espanto laugh.

"That's true. This is unusual circumstances, but I called you both here to offer my complementary assistance in fixing your situation. What transpired recently is a travesty and I want to help make things right," replies Sato.

"Thank you," says Jessica.

"Mahalo," says Gina. She then adds, "Detective Kameda recommended we speak to you and he wants you to call him after our meeting."

Sato smiles, "Him and I just talked to each other on the phone a few minutes ago, but I'll call him again after this meeting. Lopaka is my good friend from Maui High School. We played baseball together at Maui High. We won an island championship my senior year."

Gina says, "I lived on Maui most of my life. I went to King Kekaulike." (High School.)

Sato says, "Oh that's cool. I miss Maui. I go there 2-3 times a year to visit my parents in Kahului. Maui's just so much more peaceful and laid back compared to O'ahu."

"It is. I go back every few months to see my family in Ha'ikū," says Gina.

"Ha'ikū's a beautiful place. That's good of you that you see your family. Family is important...Anyways, can I see your contracts?"

Jessica and Gina hand Sato their 14 page contracts. Sato quickly observes that they are both exactly the same. Sato quickly reads through one of the contracts.

Sato says, "This is a very complicated contract to understand, but it's a model release contract. It gives Mr. Smith 100% rights over the photos to do what he wants with it, including printing them, uploading them onto the internet, using them for commercial use or even selling them. On page 11, the contract says, in very confusing and complicated wording, that he has 100% ownership rights of the photos."

Jessica sighs in anger.

Gina, dejected, says, "Detective Kameda mentioned basically the same thing."

Sato says, "I'm sure he did. Photographers usually have a person sign this type of contract if they are paying a model for work, with the clear understanding that the model is signing all their rights away and the photographer or employer of the photographer can do what they want with it. It's beyond unusual for a client to pay a photographer to take their photos and then sign a model release contract like this giving the photographer 100% rights. In other words, this particular contract is the type of contract a model would sign knowing their photos were going to be placed in a magazine or internet site. This is gross misapplication to have this contract for people like you two."

Jessica starts to cry. Sato grabs a tissue box from his desk and hands it to Jessica.

Jessica says, "My husband Franklin is going to freak out if he hears about this."

Sato says, "I'm sorry."

"Me too," says Amelia.

Jessica sighs.

Sato says, "Look we have hope here. It's obvious Wesley grossly misled you both in this model release contract. He obviously should have known better as a professional photographer. We can file a lawsuit to fight for ownership rights. We have a fairly good case especially with the very confusing and misleading language on page 11. I can tell you that this contract wasn't written by a lawyer. If it was, they need to be disbarred."

Jessica says, "Thank you."

Gina asks, "But what do we do about our photos that are on at least three internet sites?"

Sato says, "I was actually just about to speak on that. I can send you both a digital letter with my letterhead on it saying that a lawsuit is pending on ownership rights and you want your nude photos permanently taken down off their site. You can send one to each internet site that have your nude photos posted with the hopes that the company or individual will comply and take your photos down. More than likely they will. Companies don't want trouble or potential lawsuits put on them.

"If an internet site gives you trouble and doesn't take down your photos within a couple of weeks after you sent them this letter, let me know and I'll send you a much stronger letter or contact them myself. And by the way, don't worry about paying me for this meeting or the help I am offering you. I just want to help you both in this rough situation. Plus, Yuki would kill me if I charged you guys."

Both women smile a little, then thank Sato.

Sato says, "If Wesley Smith isn't his legal or professional name, then that may be another way the contract could be voided as well."

"I see," says Gina.

"That would be great if that were the case," Jessica adds. She starts to tear up again. Gina tears up a little as well.

Espanto steps into the conversation and says, "I'd like to say that photography has a lot of gray areas concerning ownership rights and different states have different laws on the books. The main thing to understand is that when a person snaps a photo of you with their camera and equipment, such as a school photographer, even though the photo is an image or picture of you, that doesn't mean you own that picture.

The school photographer has ownership of the photos and can sell it to you or not.

"Sometimes they have you sign a model release and sometimes they don't. So this example is why it's important to talk to a photographer and find out what the ownership rights are and read the contracts if they have them. Professional photographers should always have a contract on hand. If they don't, then a judge would probably side with the photographer on ownership rights."

Sato adds, "It's also important that if a photographer or anyone presents you a contract, read through it so there is no gray area. Concerning ownership, if you want 100% ownership rights of your photos, you want to have a 'work for hire' contract where the photographer takes your photos as an independent contractor and you own the photos. You need to spell this out clearly in a contract, that you might have to type up yourself, that the photographer will take the photos, but you, the client, will retain 100% ownership rights of the photos. Some photographers may want some photos for their portfolio, but that's up to the client in a work for hire type of contract if you want to give this permission or not."

Espanto says, "Like myself, I do photography as a part-time business on the weekends. Sometimes, I have clients that want to take semi-nude or nude photos. In the past, I took nude photos of both men and women, but now that I'm engaged, I agreed with Clarence to take nude photographs of women only. For any photo shoot I take, I have simple easy to read contracts. If they ask about ownership rights, which only happens once in a while, I explain to them that as a rule, since it's my camera and my equipment, the ownership rights are to the photographer who takes the photos and creates the intellectual property of the photo. Most people are okay with this."

Gina says, "Huh."

Jessica exclaims, "Wow."

Espanto continues, "The ones who insist on 100% ownership rights, which have only been a couple of people, I offer a simple one page work for hire contract where for a little bit more money, I take the photos, but they will have 100% ownership rights of the photos. I'll edit them, send it to them, then let them know I'm deleting the photos off my memory card and computer once they 100% confirm that they got all the photos. I'll send them an email the next day to double check that they have all the photos before I delete them off my memory card and computer."

Gina says, "I see."

Espanto continues, "On one occasion, a woman signed with me a work for hire contract and then handed me their memory card and camera. I took the photos, checking them frequently as I shoot for quality, then I handed her back the camera after the shoot was done. I was fine with that actually because the fun part for me is the actual shooting of the photos and not the editing and emailing. She edited her photos herself. I asked her politely for a few non-nude shots for my own portfolio, but she didn't give me any of them. That's the way it is sometimes."

Jessica says, "Before meeting Wesley Smith, I really thought that if I pay someone to take my photos, I own them."

Espanto says, "Again, by law, the photographer or in some cases, the employer of the photographer, usually ends up as the owner of the photos since they are the creator of the intellectual work, especially if it's their camera and equipment they are using. They might grant you rights to post them, use them, maybe even duplicate them, but they still own the photos."

Jessica says, "This photography business is a lot more complicated then I thought."

Indecent Photographer

Espanto says, "It is. The overwhelming majority of photographers are honest and good people. They would not do what Wesley did to you. Most photographers I know would not post nude photos on the internet or sell or give someone photos to someone else like Wesley appears to have done, but just like any job, there are good and bad in every profession. One or two rotten apples can spoil the whole barrel. Now I do know a couple of male photographers that like going around showing their friends or other photographers some of their photos they took, including nude photos of women, but I don't know of cases, other than this case, where they gave or sold nude photos to people or posted them without the consent of the person."

Gina says, "Unbelievable."

Gina asks Sato, "So hypothetically, what if in the past, an ex-husband took nude photos of a now ex-wife, does he own the photos even after a divorce?"

Sato says, "That's probably something a judge would have to sort out, but a smart woman would take those photos and get them away from the ex-husband as quick as possible. And who owns the camera and memory card could also come into play. If it was her camera and memory card, she then could easily say that it's her photos because it's her equipment, but the laws are not always that black and white. And they vary from state to state. Some states actually have little or practically no laws concerning photography. "

Gina says, "That's terrible."

Sato continues, "I agree...Now there are laws on the books that say a person can't just post semi-nude or nude photos of you without the person's consent, unless there is a model release type of contract in play. They could be held criminally or civilly liable, but as you know, that doesn't stop people from posting or showing nude photos and creating damage to the person's reputation.

Gina says, "In my case, my ex-husband would take my camera and sneak up on me in the shower. He would snap it without my permission and show it to me later. It was really creepy."

Espanto says, "What a jerk."

Gina adds, "This was part of the reason we got divorced and part of the reason I took my photos and memory cards back before he could claim them."

Sato says, "Smart."

Jessica says, "This makes me realize that if you want to make sure you own your photo, take a selfie or take a nude photo in the mirror or take a photo with your own camera phone using a camera stand."

Sato says, "Honestly, that's not a bad idea. Some camera phones now-a-days actually take better photos than some traditional cameras on the market. And some have excellent editing software built in the phone, so you could instantly edit your own photo right then and there."

Espanto jokingly says, "Shh. Don't give anyone any ideas, that kind of talk could put me out of business. I need the extra money."

Espanto laughs a little to herself. Gina and Jessica smile a little, but they are not in a playful mood.

Jessica says, "I should of had you (Espanto) take my nude photos. I just didn't know you did this type of photography."

Espanto replies, "I guess I need to advertise better, but if you need my services in the future, here's my card."

Espanto hands both Jessica and Gina her photography business cards.

Both Jessica and Gina thank her.

Gina asks Sato, "What's going to happen to Terrence, Jerry and anyone else that passed our nude photos around work?"

Sato answers, "I can't answer that right now because we just started investigating today."

Gina angrily says, "I see, but just so you know, I want to see people fired for this, especially Terrence and Jerry. I'm very upset and embarrassed that my co-workers and friends have seen me nude not by my choice."

Jessica adds, "I'm very upset too. It really sucks that so many people were viewing our naked photos and no one came to tell us until Amanda found out last night and told us about them."

Espanto adds, "I understand how you feel. I would be angry as well if any of my nude photos I took when I was younger were shown to my co-workers."

Sato, surprised, asks, "What did you say?"

Espanto, realizing she said something she didn't want Clarence to know, says, "Um...Let's talk about that later please."

Gina, changing the focus of the conversation, asks Sato, "Can we go after Terrence and Jerry criminally?"

"I'm a corporate lawyer and don't practice criminal law, so you should call Detective Kameda and ask him that question. I believe you can go after them in civil court, but again, call him. I'll call him later today and ask him to assist you both in taking down your nude photos off of websites, but again, please contact these companies on your own using the letter I will e-mail you guys later today. Don't rely on Kameda, I know he has a lot on his plate concerning his criminal case load. Crime doesn't take days off. I'll also see if he can have the police pick up Wesley Smith and have a serious chat with him. Maybe Kameda can convince Mr. Smith to void your contracts so we can avoid a lawsuit and a court trail."

Both women thank Sato and Espanto. They continue a little small talk before leaving Sato's office. As they are driving home, Gina and Jessica discuss talking to another lawyer about possibly suing the hospital because of what happened with their nude photos over a two week period. Gina is a little hesitant and not sure if she wants to go that route, but Jessica is not. Jessica is really thinking seriously about it, especially since she's still figuring out how to tell her husband what happened.

CHAPTER 10

Epilogue

A day after Jessica and Gina met Clarence Sato and Amelia Espanto in Sato's office, Detective Kameda had Terrence brought into the police station for questioning. With Terrence's lawyer, Terrence made a deal to explain everything to Detective Kameda. Terrence said that he purchased the photos from a man named Philip. Terrence also said that he had no idea where Philip got the photos, except that he got the photos from a local photographer. In addition, Terrence said that he suspects Philip might have child pornography on his computer, because he once saw a file on his computer labelled, "Southeast Asian girls" and when he asked Philip about it, Philip said it was nothing and quickly changed the subject. Terrence gave Detective Kameda Philip's dark web address where he sells photos of nude women, from Hawai'i, to European based clients in English, German, Spanish, Russian and the French language.

The Honolulu Police Department talked to the FBI and partnered together with them on this investigation. The FBI got a warrant to do surveillance on Philip. Detective Kameda discovered that Philip had an account, like Terrence said, selling nude photos of Hawai'i women. The FBI also found a deeper Dark Web site of Philip's selling child pornography he bought from Wesley. The FBI brought in Philip for questioning and tracked down hundreds of buyers of Philip's child porn, which were both in America, Europe and from around the world.

Philip, under legal advisement, made a plea deal to testify against Wesley. Philip got ten years in prison, instead of a whole lot more, for his cooperation. The FBI found Wesley in Upstate, New York. They pretended to be Philip on the internet and asked to buy more child pornography. Wesley wasn't surprised that Philip wanted more photos. He tapped into his Southeast Asian contacts and got more underaged photos for "Philip."

When Wesley made a deal with "Philip" and sent the photos after receiving Bitcoin, the FBI picked up Wesley in New York and prosecuted him there. Wesley stood trial and was sentenced to life in prison with a chance at parole in 15 years. More than his 70 years could handle. He died at age 73 in prison from a heart attack. (As part of a deal, Wesley voided all his model release photography contracts, including Gina and Jessica's contracts. He also helped in the prosecution of his Southeast Asian contact.) The contact, an American living in Cambodia, was murdered in prison before he could stand trail.

After Terrence got fired, he got a job as a dishwasher and made a little less than he did as a transporter. He would rather be a transporter, but knew he couldn't show his face in the hospital he got fired at. He had too many enemies there that despised him for what he did to Jessica and Gina.

Negotiated by his lawyer, in exchange for Terrence's testimony that led to Philip and Wesley getting arrested and sentenced, Jessica and Gina didn't pursue Terrence criminally or civilly. They also didn't pursue Jerry criminally or civilly either.

After Jerry got fired, he worked under the table for his wife's care home that took care of four elderly patients that were medically sick. A year later, he switched over to becoming a Taxi driver working long hours. Like Terrence, he missed working in the hospital as a transporter.

Indecent Photographer

No one ever found out that it was Jerry who first put Gina and Jessica's nude photos on three internet sites, along with other Hawai'i women. From there, strangers on the internet would copy and paste the photos and post it on other sites. This is the reason why Gina and Jessica's photos would continuously spread from one site to another. It was also the reason why women from Hawai'i started filing complaints with the police against Wesley.

Jessica and Gina filed a lawsuit against the hospital. They got a quick out of court settlement worth a fair amount of money. As part of the speedy settlement, brokered by Clarence Sato, they both signed a non-disclosure agreement, which meant they were not to speak about this case again, both in public and private. The hospital didn't want negative publicity that could hurt the hospital's reputation and bottom line.

Jessica didn't feel comfortable being around so many people that saw her nude photos. She got a full-time day shift job at a nearby hospital on a cardiac floor. Gina stayed and as part of the settlement, became an educational nurse with hourly pay, a large pay raise and union protection. She loved her new Monday to Friday day shift hours with all weekends and hospital recognized holidays off.

Jessica and Gina's photos were later found on dozens of sites on the regular web and Dark Web. They did their best to take down as much as they could, but when they took one down, another set of photos of them appeared on another site. After awhile, they gave up trying to take them down. They realized that once you have a nude photo up in the internet universe, that photo might just grow legs and travel.

Jessica told her husband Franklin Tanner about what happened in an e-mail a few days after Jessica and Gina spoke to Clarence Sato and Detective Kameda. She asked for forgiveness. Surprisingly to her, Franklin forgave her and wasn't too upset, but was more concerned for his wife's mental status. He felt sorrow for Jessica and her friend Gina. When he got back, he was just happy that he was going to be a future father and treated Jessica with the respect and love she deserved. Jessica had a baby girl and named Gina as her Godmother. A few years later, Jessica and Franklin had a son. They named Gina as his Godmother too.

Since Gina did photography as a hobby in the past, she decided to open up her own photography side business. She specialized in nude photography for both men and women and took clients on the weekends she didn't have custody of Nalu. Her contracts were all work for hire contracts and she gave 100% ownership rights to the clients. She also kept things confidential. Her business grew to the point that she had long waiting lists for her time. She later found a Polynesian/Caucasian boyfriend a few months later that eventually led to marriage and children.

Both Jessica and Gina started contacting local state representatives, as well as national House of Representatives and Senators about photography laws. Jessica and Gina were pushing for laws that state if you pay a person to take your photos, the client hiring the photographer should automatically have the ownership rights of the photos and not the photographer. A couple of female politicians were interested in the proposal, including a national female senator who took nude photos in the distant past and didn't know the law the way she thought she did. She was worried that one day her nude photos might come to light. She was thankful Jessica and Gina had brought this nude photography issue to her attention.

Amanda won her match in Hawai'i and was invited into a professional fighting league in Asia. While still living and training in Hawai'i, she fought in Asia professionally for four years, amassing a record of 4-3-1 and being seen by millions of people. The money was good as well.

After her second serious concussion in Asia, she ended her career as a professional MMA fighter and went back to school to become a respiratory therapist at Kapi'olani Community College. She now works for the same hospital she started off in as a nursing assistant. She got married to an African-American/Caucasian nurse practitioner from the hospital, but they could not have children of their own. They ended up adopting two sons after medical treatments didn't seem to work. One of their sons came from an African country and the other was a mixed-Asian foster child from Hawai'i.

Yuki went back to college and became a registered nurse. She got an RN position on the same orthopedic floor she worked on as a certified nurses aide. Yuki later married a Chinese-American orthopedic doctor and had another daughter. Her husband got along just fine with her child Mia, which was very important to Yuki.

Even though Jessica works at a different hospital, the four women find time to spend together every so often. Since they all have families now, they plan a get together at a restaurant, beach or one of their houses at least once a month. The incident of what happened to Jessica and Gina is still painful, but as time goes on, the pain starts to fade and feels a little less painful each year that goes by.

Author's Bibliography: Frank Pōmaika'i Munden

Frank Pōmaika'i Munden was born on O'ahu, Hawai'i in 1971 and raised on Maui. A product of Ha'ikū Elementary School, Munden graduated from Maui High School in 1989. After some time in the US Navy as a Machinist Mate onboard the USS Arkansas CGN-41, Munden returned to Maui for several years before moving to Makiki, O'ahu in 1996.

Munden attended Kapi'olani Community College and then later, the University of Hawai'i at Mānoa where he obtained a BA in History with a minor in Political Science in 2008 and later a Post Baccalaureate in Special Education in 2011. (Munden took a handful of classes from Maui Community College, (Now University of Hawai'i Maui College), Honolulu Community College, and Chaminade University of Honolulu.)

Munden spent time as a special education history teacher for the Hawai'i Department of Education. Currently, he's in a Nursing Assistant at a major hospital on O'ahu.

Munden is a Christian who believes in racial equality and fairness in life. His favorite music genres are old school Reggae, like Bob Marley, Hawaiian and Christian rap.

Munden got his name Pōmaika'i from his first Hawaiian language class by his teacher, Kumu Puhi Adams. The Hawaiian word translates to blessed or blessing from Heaven.

Munden has a girlfriend named Jenell "Ke'alohi" Sato. Munden's youngest brother, Frazier Munden lives on Maui. His other brother, Forest Munden, lives in Canada with his girlfriend, Catherine "Cat" Chan. His father, Frank Munden Sr., (RIP), passed away peacefully on Maui on October 24, 2021. His mother, Faith Munden (RIP), passed away peacefully on Maui on February 25, 2022.

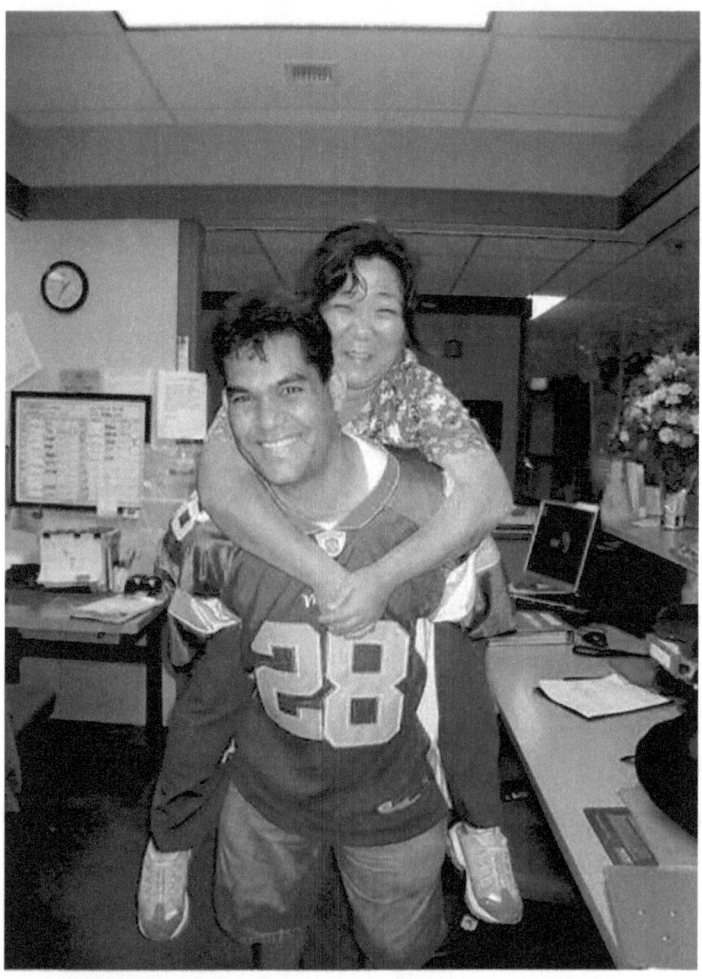

Frank Pōmaika'i Munden and Jenell Sato. Makiki, O'ahu, Hawai'i 2010.

Illustrator's Bibliography: Andy Lee

Andy Lee was born in Hong Kong in 1974, but raised in the United States. He graduated from Punahou High School in Honolulu, Hawai'i in 1992. He obtained a BFA in Illustration with a minor in Biology from Washington University in St. Louis, Missouri in 1996. Later, he got a Post Baccalaureate in Secondary Education from the University of Hawai'i at Mānoa in 2008.

Lee is currently a teacher at a local high school on O'ahu. He lives with his wife, Cindy, daughter, Emma and father, Henry.

Lee has worked in Chicago, St. Louis, Atlanta and Honolulu, Hawai'i. He has done work for Marvel, DC Comics, LeBron James (Nike) and many other companies and individuals.

Lee helped Frank Munden with three books:"Tamehameha Uncensored Detailed Histories of Hawai'i's First King"; "Love is Deeper Than Skin" and "The Central American Drug Ship US Navy: 1990." These books can be found on Amazon by typing the title of the book and Frank Munden.

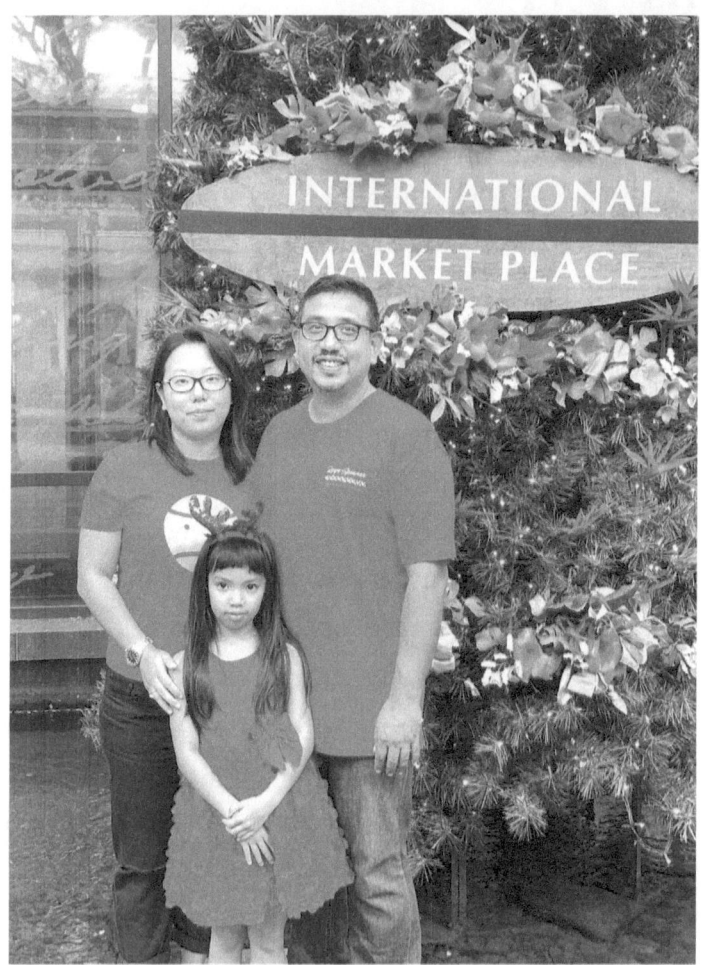

Left to Right: Cindy Lee, Emma Lee and Andy Lee. Waikīkī, O'ahu, Hawai'i 2018.

Editor: Pam Calilao

Pam Calilao was born in 1972 on the island of Lana'i and was raised there. She graduated from Lana'i High and Elementary School in 1990. Shortly after graduating, she moved to the island of O'ahu. Calilao successfully managed a national shoe store franchise for over 20 years, while obtaining an Associates Degree in Applied Science-Health Information Technology from Heald College in 2013.

Later, she obtained an Associate of Applied Science in Healthcare Administration, Billing and Coding from Hawai'i Medical College in 2021. In addition, she recently got certified as a professional coder in 2021.

Calilao is currently in management at a local nursing home on O'ahu. She has four children. Among Calilao's hobbies, she likes spending time with family and friends, as well as going to the beach.

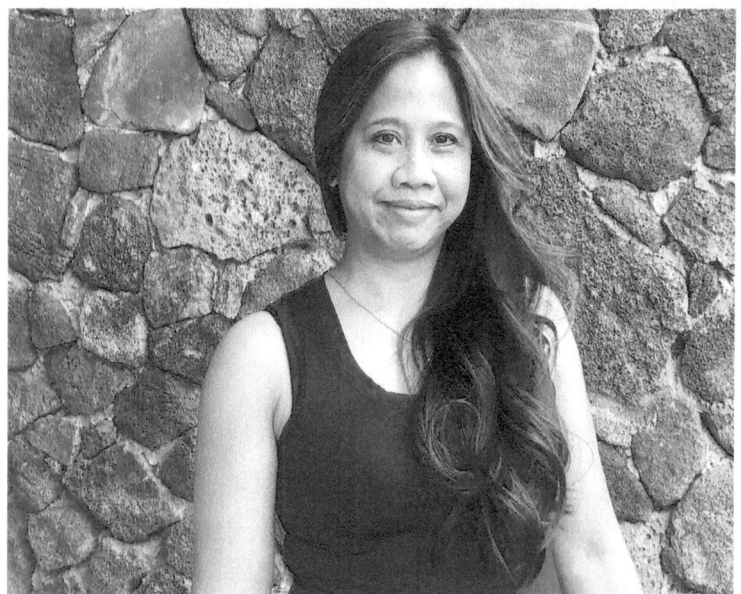

Pam Calilao. Makiki, O'ahu, Hawai'i. 2021.

Editor: James Giroux

James Giroux was born in Costa Rica and currently lives on Maui with his wife Krista. He attended Ha'ikū Elementary School and Maui High School with Frank Munden. He graduated from Maui High School in 1989.

Giroux graduated from the University of Hawai'i at Mānoa with a BA in English. He later graduated with a Juris Doctorate Degree from California Western Law School in California. He practiced Criminal Law and Administrative Law in Hawai'i. He worked for the State of Hawai'i Office of the Public Defender and County of Maui Office of Corporation Counsel.

Giroux retired after surviving a plane crash on the island of Lana'i while serving as Deputy Corporation Counsel assigned to the Lana'i Planning Commission.

Giroux appeared in a couple of Frank Munden's YouTube amateur films that can be found on the Youtube channel, "Ohana Production Group."

Giroux has a son named Jacob, who lives on Maui.

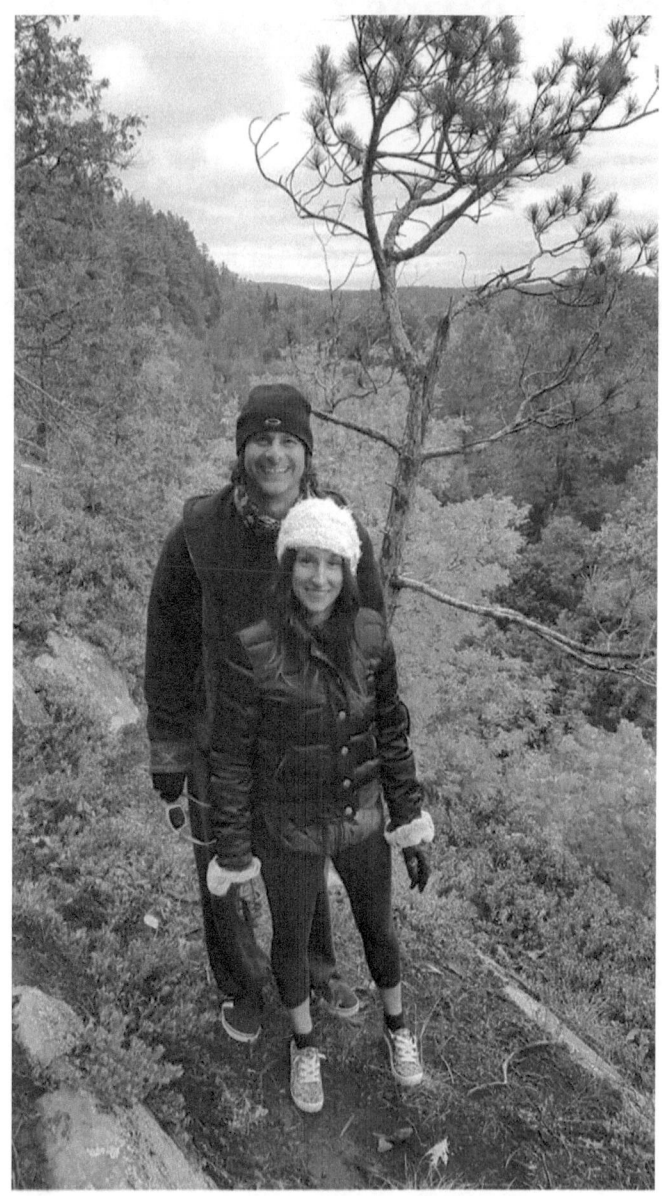

James Giroux and his wife Krista Dawn Giroux.

Editor: Bo Daniel Mandoe

Bo Daniel Mandoe was born and raised on the island of Maui. He attended St. Anthony Catholic grade school and junior high, winning the Catholic Schools Spelling Bee in 1988 and 1989. In 1994, Mandoe graduated from Seabury Hall Prepatory Academy and shocked everyone from his parents, to the school administration, by foregoing college and becoming a pastry and bread baker.

Six years later, weary of the restaurant life, he began attending Portland Community College, graduating in 2002 with an Associate of Arts Degree. Between the years of 2005-2006 he attended Portland State University, studying book publishing with the school's prestigious Ooligan Press.

For the past fifteen years, Mandoe has supported his family and dream of becoming a published writer through carpentry and woodworking. He has written numerous blogs and is currently working on a young adult novel about a hypothetical virtual future.

Mandoe has a daughter named Eva and a cat named Lightning.

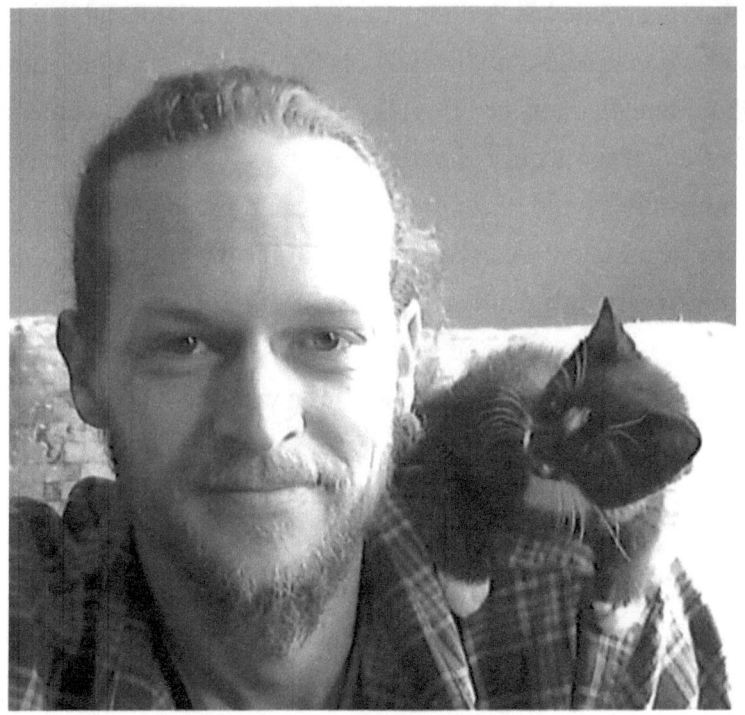

Bo Daniel Mandoe and his cat Lightning.

Editor: Angel (Garcia) Wyatt

Angel (Garcia)Wyatt was born in Sulpher Springs, Texas in 1985 and raised in Dallas. She graduated from Quitman ISD in 2003. Wyatt spent time in the US Army as a Preventive Medicine Specialist. She moved to Hawai'i in 2008.

Wyatt obtained a Sociology Degree with a minor in Psychology in 2016 and a Masters in Forensic Psychology in 2018 from Chaminade University of Honolulu. Currently, she works as a Intensive Training Specialist in Virginia.

Wyatt appeared in several of Frank Munden's Youtube films that can be found on the Youtube channel, "Ohana Production Group."

Wyatt has a husband named Teddy Wyatt and a son named Marko Garcia.

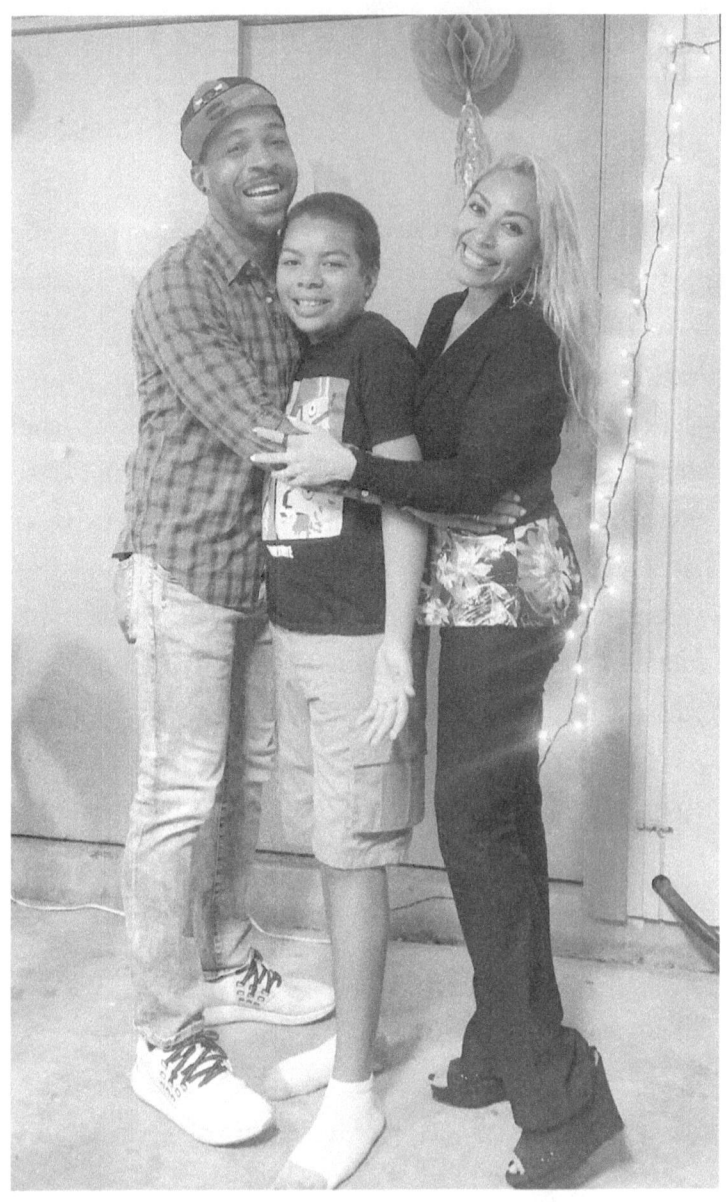

Left to right: Teddy Wyatt, Marko Garcia and Angel (Garcia) Wyatt. 2020.

Author's Last Words

Munden wrote this book based off a blending of true stories he personally witnessed in his life. Munden has several friends in the photography business, both here in Hawai'i and the US Mainland. He's generally familiar with the in's and out's of professional photography.

Munden felt that this book needed to be written. He felt it's important that people know that photography is not just a black and white business. Munden wants people to know that when they take a photograph, they should know who has the ownership rights of the photo, especially if they take nude photos. People need to read and fully understand the contract before they take off their clothing and pose for photos. (A work for hire contract clearly stating who owns the photos is a way to spell out ownership, however, just taking nude selfies is a more guaranteed way of ensuring that you own your photos.)

Munden made an amateur YouTube movie called, "Overexposed X3." This 16 minute short film is loosely based off of this book, "Indecent Photographer." Munden dreams that this book could be made into a real feature length film. Overexposed X3 can be found on the YouTube channel, "Ohana Production Group." (Editor Angel Wyatt plays Jessica in the film and editor James Giroux plays a lawyer in the film.)

Special Thanks

Special thanks to: Pam Calilao; Katherine Chan; James Giroux; Kirsta Dawn Giroux, Taylor Meleana Ka'aiakamanu King; Andy Lee; Cindy Lee; Bo Daniel Mandoe; Faith Munden (RIP); Forest Munden; Frank Munden Sr. (RIP); Frazier Munden; Kandice Symister; Jenell "Ke'alohi" Sato and Angel (Garcia) Wyatt.

Print book and e-books by Frank Pōmaika'i Munden on Amazon.

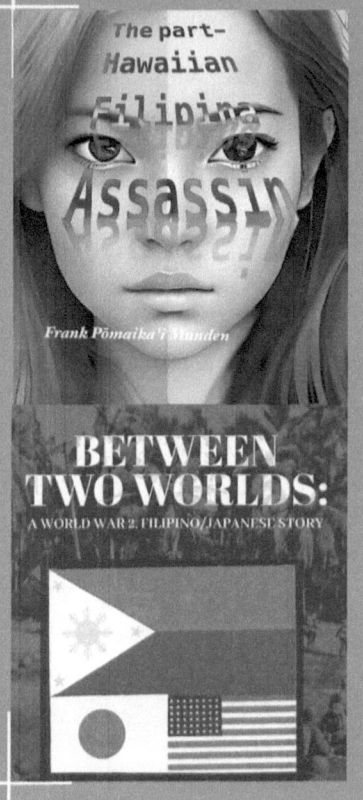

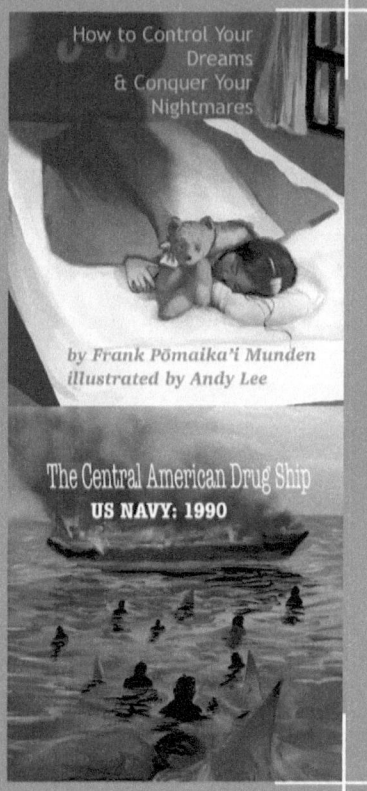

www.ingramcontent.com/pod-product-compliance
Lightning Source LLC
Chambersburg PA
CBHW020447220526
45464CB00002B/888